King's Drive Days

My childhood in 1950s Fulwood

by

Francis Mohan

To my dear cousin Monika, with love from Francis

© **Francis Mohan 2023**

Kindle Direct Publishing

ISBN: 9798856862941

For my brother Maurice

CONTENTS

Foreword

At 70 years of age, in 2022, I decided that I would finally try to do something that I had always wanted to do, which was to jot down on paper the remaining thoughts and memories I had of my childhood years. Our eldest grandchild Henry is now 10 years old. It is strange and sobering to think that the years that I am describing in this book are the same years that Henry has already lived through, his from 2013 to 2023, mine from '52 to '62.

I am very aware of the tricks that memory can play, so I do not claim to have set down an accurate or true record of things that happened to me and to my family. Even if what I have said is accurate, it only represents a fraction of our life, a few snapshots, like the photos included in the text. When our mother was 70, she gifted each of her seven children with an album containing a carefully chosen selection of original family photographs. It is from that album that I have chosen the images included in this book. The trouble is that these few written memories, together with those few photographs, turn into the official history, simply because there is nothing else to access. On the other hand, I have often wished that Dad could have written, or even told us more, about his childhood years.

The 1950s have always been a source of nostalgia and I know that there are risks in overly sentimental reminiscence. The 1950s are also a battleground in debates over what was good and healthy, and what was dangerous and destructive, in our national culture.

I am also very much aware that my brothers and sisters could each provide different accounts of those early years. I am not able to provide any information or insight into their experiences in Cambridge, or Stocks Road, or Preston Catholic College or Winckley Square. More importantly, every child has their own unique relationship with their parents, as well as with each of their siblings.

I would therefore like to apologise for anything I have written that my brothers and sisters might not be happy with and I hope they will correct me wherever they can. This little memoir must of its nature be flawed and incomplete. Nevertheless, here, for better or for worse, are my few memories of those far-off, ever-present, King's Drive days. Having committed them to print, my overwhelming feeling is one of gratitude for all that I was given in the most formative years of my life.

Bewdley
September 2023

Chapter 1

Fitzwilliam College, Cambridge

And a little brown jug

Dad is holding a baby, with Mum by his side. The picture must have been taken in 1948, the year in which Edmund was born on 12th January, almost exactly nine months after their wedding day. Mum is a picture of 1940s elegance, in a beautiful, dark, tailored suit with padded shoulders. The jacket is gathered in at the waist, then splays out. Her hair is done in 1940s film-star style. Dad wears a smart black suit of capacious cut. His head inclines affectionately and proudly towards his first child, his son Edmund. There is a smart black car behind them. They are starting their family life together. Their black hair shines. He is a student. She has no work. But they look normal, prosperous, well turned out.

The most treasured image of Dad is his official army portrait. He is very handsome, with his dark, swept-back hair and his strong features. His battledress is immaculate. The khaki shirt has a smart, button-down collar. On his shoulder we see that he is a member of the Royal Signals. On his arm, the single stripe of a lance-corporal. Above it, and below the Signals sign, is the black bull on a yellow background, the emblem of the 11th Armoured Brigade. Dad has smiling eyes, a serene expression, and something of a smile playing around his lips. He looks confident, but sensitive.

They were not something any of us had ever seen, or could remember, but the Threadbare Corduroy Trousers were a cultural reference point for Dad. They were, according to him, all he had to wear for many years of his early married life and teaching career. They were all he could afford. The cord was worn off at the knees and the seat. But it didn't worry him. He was happy to be poor. Or at least resigned to his lot. He was a teacher. It was the 1940s and 1950s. He had leather patches on his elbows. They all did. Humble. Unpretentious. Dad also loved his army shorts. These were very loose fitting and baggy and they tightened at the waist with a pair of buckle straps. They were the sort that featured in the film *Bridge Over the River Kwai*. Dad wore them on our early camping trips. Like camping itself, Dad's army shorts were for him a symbol of freedom from the shackles of work and the conventions of daily life.

After the war, Dad met up with a former army friend, who told him about a scheme to support demobbed veterans obtaining degrees. The Minister of Labour and National Service decreed in 1946 that 90% of the undergraduate places at Cambridge were to be allocated to ex-servicemen. Dad's college, Fitzwilliam, already had a long history of opening up access to the University of Cambridge for students who would otherwise not have been able to afford it. Since late Victorian times it had been possible to enrol at Cambridge without becoming a member of a college. Living expenses at Cambridge were much lower for a non-collegiate student. All such non-collegiate students were eventually enrolled at Fitzwilliam Hall, named after the row of Georgian terraced houses in Fitzwilliam Street in which the students were housed and received some of their teaching. Until the Second World War, Fitzwilliam had the status of a university department rather than that of a college. It was realised after the war that new premises would have to be built if collegiate status was ever to be achieved. The transition from non-collegiate to full Cambridge college status was largely achieved by Walter Grave, a Fitzwilliam administrator and don who was familiar to Dad from his time at the college.

Dad was always very loyal to the memory of Fitzwilliam and proud that two of his sons went on to receive their university education there. He loved the academic work and had plenty of men of his own age and background as fellow students. In addition to the black / grey terraces in Fitzwilliam Street, the college occupied 30 / 31 Trumpington Street, an elegant early eighteenth-century mansion with a fine classical doorcase fronting onto Trumpington Street. Just up the road from Fitzwilliam, at 52 Trumpington Street, was the famous Fitzbillies tea shop, which Dad and his friends used to frequent. Fitzbillies had been founded in the 1920s and was famous for its Chelsea buns.

One of the biggest influences on Dad during his time at Cambridge was Alfred Newman Gilbey, the priest in charge of the Roman Catholic Chaplaincy at Fisher House. Dad would often talk about Monsignor Gilbey and how much he had loved him and learned from him. Gilbey was a legendary figure at Cambridge throughout his long tenure of the chaplaincy, from 1932 to 1965.

He was a graduate of Trinity College Cambridge, and every year a Mass is still celebrated for the repose of his soul. He was known and respected across the whole university as a cultured and courteous gentleman who could quietly articulate the Catholic faith. Throughout the time that Dad was at Cambridge, Gilbey fought, and won, a gruelling battle to prevent Fisher House from being demolished to make way for the new Lion Yard shopping development.

While Dad was an undergraduate, accommodation in Cambridge was in very short supply. The total number of university students at that time, around 6000, was the highest it had ever been in the university's history. Also, Cambridge had become during the war a huge centre for Civil Service departments moved out of London, which put further pressure on accommodation. Mum and Dad once went for a walk outside Cambridge and stopped at a farm. The farm had a sort of barn or outhouse.

1940s portrait of Mum

Dad took one look at it and thought it would be a wonderful place for them to start their married life together. They bravely knocked on the farmhouse door and inquired whether the farmer could take a lodger. The farmer was very polite and looked at them with pity and sympathy in his eyes, but said 'I'm sorry, but you couldn't possibly live in there.' There was no heat, electricity, water, or toilet.

Victorious servicemen returning to their home country were rewarded in 1947 by one of the coldest winters in British history. During January and February temperatures dropped to as low as -20 degrees centigrade. Food rations were lower even than they had been during the war, winter crops were frozen into the ground, factories had to close and blackouts were frequent. March brought terrible snowstorms, closely followed by widespread flooding and the breaching of the dykes around East Anglia. But April brought a wedding.

The Church of Our Lady of the Assumption and the English Martyrs, stands on one corner of the huge road junction of Hills Road and Lensfield Road on the southern edge of the university area. It is a vast Gothic Revival edifice, with an enormous spire that can be seen from miles around. It was built between 1885 and 1890 by a very famous architect called Edward Joseph Hansom. Inside the nave, over the entrance to the chancel, hangs a huge rood, with Mary and John picked out in vivid reds and blues, and above them a striking risen Christ with arms outstretched, in priestly robes and golden crown.

It was beneath this awe-inspiring sculpture that Mum and Dad were married. One day, long in the future, one of their granddaughters would marry in a magnificent ceremony just a few hundred yards away at Trinity College Cambridge, with hundreds of guests and a lavish reception beneath the portraits of the kings in the Trinity Great Hall. On 9th April 1947, the impoverished ex-serviceman married his bride. It was her 24th birthday. There was neither wedding dress nor wedding guests nor wedding presents nor wedding reception. The officiating priest had to tell the young couple that the marriage could not be solemnised without a witness. They went out onto the street outside the church and collared a passer-by, a lady, who agreed to act as witness. The wedding breakfast, such as it was, took place at the Lyons Tea Shop on Petty Cury. Mum and Dad had embarked on the four decades they would have together. A surprise and very precious wedding gift did in fact materialise in the form of a little brown earthenware jug, which the lady witness had managed to fetch in a hurry from her home.

The first accommodation the newly-weds had was in a basement with a cement floor. Dad managed to buy a bottle of wine to cheer them up and help them to celebrate. While removing the cork form the bottle Dad's hand slipped. The bottle smashed on the floor and its precious contents were lost as they splashed onto everything in sight. Mum and Dad put their arms around each other and wept. One day Dad staggered into their flat, the proud bearer of an industrial-sized sack of oats that he had somehow acquired on the cheap. At least they would now be able to start each day with a nourishing breakfast. Within days the oats went mouldy and had to be thrown away.

While living in Cambridge Mum and Dad found work at a prison camp for German prisoners of war. The most likely location of their camp would be the Trumpington Prisoner of War Camp, Camp 45, a camp which held Italian and German prisoners of war until late 1948, by which time almost all prisoners of war had been repatriated. Their work at the camp must have taken place during the summers of 1947 and / or 1948. They were very well suited to this work. They were very kind to the prisoners, who loved them back in return. There was a need for agricultural workers in the area. By the end of the year all German prisoners of war had been repatriated. While living in Cambridge, Mum also found work at the Pye factory, Pye Radio Ltd, on St Andrew's Road in Chesterton. One day some of the engineers asked mum if she wanted to come into the lab to see something very special. It was the first television, a tiny screen in a huge metal box.

While they lived in Cambridge Mum and Dad's favourite Sunday activity was to go to the beautiful Botanical Gardens. Dad used to love to put Edmund in the push chair and run along with him. The eldest three of the family liked to think of themselves as a cut above, not just because they were the eldest, but because they were born in the beautiful and famous university town of Cambridge. The first-born son Edmund Anthony, born on 12th January 1948, was followed by a girl, Veronica Anne, born on 10th April 1949 and Maurice Peter, born on 18th August, 1950. Today, and even then, that would have made a perfect family for most people. But there is a saying, 'new house, new baby'.

Born in Cambridge: Veronica, Maurice, and Edmund

Chapter 2

St Philip's School, Birmingham

And a prayer to Our Lady

Mum and Dad had only four years in Cambridge. By 1951, Dad had secured his first teaching post as teacher of Modern Languages at St. Philip's School, Birmingham. He started his first term at St Philip's in September 1951, when Maurice was one year old. When they moved from Cambridge, Mum was already eight weeks pregnant with me. I was born at the Birmingham Women's Hospital in Edgbaston on 21st April 1952, at around 3.30pm. I weighed 9lb.

St Philip's was on the Hagley Road in Birmingham, next to the impressive Baroque church of the Oratory of Saint Philip Neri. Squeezed in at the side of the school and church site, and leading off at a right angle from the Hagley Road, was Windsor Terrace. This 'street' had no vehicular access and the houses were accessed by a pedestrian pathway. In this secluded terrace stood three pairs of white stuccoed houses, built around 1840 and Grade II listed by Historic England. When Mum and Dad lived there, they were pretty run down and were almost certainly owned by St Philip's and rented out. Living next door was another large Catholic family. In between the two properties was a hedge. Edmund, Veronica, and Maurice were aged 4, 3 and 2. They would play at taking Dad's tools and passing them through the hedge to the children on the other side, who were of a similar but slightly older age. Dad would have to go round next door and beg them back, not knowing exactly what had been taken.

Although they were not there for very long, Mum and Dad were very happy in Birmingham. They liked to go for a drink at the elegant Plough and Harrow pub, adjacent to the Oratory on the corner of Monument Road. While in Birmingham, Dad gave talks to the Newman Society and attended its meetings, something I would do fifty years later. I was baptised at the Oratory, which was and remains a bastion of traditional Catholic liturgy, practice and belief, the brand of Catholicism championed by Monsignor Gilbey at Cambridge.

I was baptised at the age of four weeks, on 21st May 1952, in the magnificent font at the back of the Oratory. The priest was Fr Geoffrey Walmsley. Fr Geoffrey died rather suddenly, while serving as Provost of the Oratory.

St Philip's was a very prestigious Catholic grammar school for boys. Just around the corner was St Paul's, the respected grammar school for girls. Dad was a highly respected member of staff. When I applied for my post as Head of Sixth Form at Hagley Catholic High School in 1988, one member of the interviewing panel was the school chaplain, the Rev Fr James Holland. He was an extremely friendly and genial priest. Jim had been a pupil at St Philip's, aged around 15 or 16 when Dad was teaching there. He said to me 'When you walked into the interview room, I thought it was Frank Mohan.' Almost forty years after he had been taught by Dad, he remembered him with huge affection and respect. The same thing happened on another occasion when the Schools Liaison Officer for Newman College came to Hagley to give a talk to the Sixth Form. His name was Denis Hurley and he told me that he had been a very good friend of Dad in the couple of years Dad spent at St Philip's. When Denis saw me in the school foyer he said 'Well, I don't need to ask who you are, you're quite obviously Frank Mohan's son.' He immediately followed this with 'How's your mother?' Mum and Dad were a very strong and striking couple. People never seemed to forget them and always remembered them with immense fondness. Dad will have been aged about 34 when he secured this first teaching post, suffering from the late start to a career experienced by so many ex-servicemen. Denis was a PE teacher, a good ten years younger than Dad, a very energetic and positive personality with a vibrant and immovable Catholic faith. Every year for years Denis would ask after my mother and say what happy memories he had of those St Philip's days when he first met Mum and Dad. By a remarkable twist of fate, sixty years on from Dad's time at St. Philip's, our son Timothy was to marry Rachel, for whom Denis Hurley was a much-loved great uncle, the brother to her Nan.

While they were in Birmingham, they made a very good friend called Monica Greenie, who I think must have been a teacher and a spinster. The only thing we knew about Monica Greenie was her handwriting, a beautifully florid and artistic hand in fine blue ink, which we saw on the Christmas card she sent to Mum and Dad every year for decades, even though their sojourn there was so brief. Mum liked it very much in Birmingham and found it to be a very friendly place.

As a teacher Dad was very keen on school trips. He had a great belief in the value of getting the boys out of school so that they could see and experience things for themselves. When he was teaching at St Philip's he took a party of boys down to Cheddar Gorge. I don't know how this fitted with his role as Modern Languages teacher.

When I was a baby, at the age of about six months, I began to fade and was very ill. Dad was very worried because one day, when I was a little baby, he was holding me and he banged my head very badly on an open cupboard door. When I began to be ill, he thought it might be as a result of that knock. I was taken to Birmingham Children's Hospital with suspected meningitis. I did not get better and I was put in an isolation unit to keep me clear of infection and to keep me away from other babies.

Mum was desperate and decided that the only hope was to sprinkle me with water from Our Lady's shrine at Lourdes. At first the doctor refused to allow Mum to gain access to me but she would not take no for an answer and managed to get to me and to pray for me while praying to Our Lady and blessing me with the Lourdes water. Mum vowed that, if I pulled through, she would name her next child after St Bernadette Soubirous, the visionary child of Lourdes.

Outside the front door at 2 Windsor Terrace, Edgbaston, Birmingham

In the back garden at 2 Windsor Terrace. We are wearing the same clothes as in the previous picture, so these pictures must have been taken at the same time. The jacket Dad is wearing was pale blue and made of Harris tweed.

Chapter 3

Stocks Road, Preston

And a teacher called Ug

Bernadette Maria was born in Preston on 12th September 1953, a beautiful baby girl. Mum and Dad had been married for 6 years and 5 months. They now had five children, three boys and two girls, with a four-year age difference between the two girls. Mum must have been pregnant for 45 out of 77 months, or over half of her married life to that date. Mum and Dad had lived in Cambridge for just four years, from the year of their marriage in 1947, to the year of Dad's graduation in 1951. They lived in Birmingham for a mere two years, the two academic years 1951-1952 and 1952-1953. When Dad started his first term of teaching at St. Philip's Birmingham, Mum was already eight weeks pregnant with me. As he started his first term of teaching in Preston, just two years later, Bernadette must have been born in the first or second week of the academic year. Dad was now embarking on his new position as Head of Modern Languages at Preston Catholic College.

When we first arrived in Preston, we lived in Stocks Road. This was red-brick terraced street, on the edge of the suburb of Ashton-on-Ribble and backing onto the Lancaster Canal. The houses sat right on the road with no front gardens, but were well built and spacious. It was a half hour walk for Dad to get to work. I have almost no recollection of Stocks Road, but Edmund and Veronica were five and four when they arrived there and do have some memories. I think Mum and Dad were very happy in their first Preston home, because every often I would here it mentioned fondly at the dinner table.

My earliest memory. It is night, I am standing in my cot. I am crying. I have wet my bed. My Mum and Dad have come in and changed my clothes. They have dressed me in a girl's nightdress. I know that it is the wrong clothing for me. My mother and father are there. It is quite dark. I think there are other children in the room, but my parents do not want to wake them. I feel that they are laughing at me. They are not intending to laugh at me or to humiliate me. There is no other dry or washed pyjama or clothing available. But I feel humiliated. I feel guilty. As if I have done something wrong. I am two years old. This incident took place in Stocks Road.

Preston was a sort of Vatican City, a holy town whose name derived from the Old English word for priest. The flame of Catholic faith had been kept alive in Lancashire by recusant families throughout the period of Catholic persecution. In Preston the Church had several strongholds and citadels, the foremost of which was Preston Catholic College. This grammar school was situated in Winckley Square, a beautiful Georgian square at the heart of the old town. As a working cotton mill town Preston was not known for its attractive urban architecture. Winckley Square, however, was a Georgian gem. It had been laid out in 1801 as a residential area for the town's gentry and had a beautiful London-style park at its heart. Preston Catholic College occupied a large part of one side of the square and had a large imposing Victorian entrance. I was very jealous of Edmund, and later Maurice, who both had the privilege of attending this school and receiving a first-class education. They also had the privilege of wearing the beautiful light green Harris Tweed jacket with leather coated buttons. The only thing I dreaded about going to this famous Jesuit college was the Tickling Slab. According to my elder brothers, in one corner of the yard was a sloping surface of rock on which all new entrants were held down and tortured by being tickled almost to the point of death.

The female counterpart of Preston Catholic College and another bastion of Catholicism, was the girls' convent school. It was situated on the other side of the Winckley Square from the Jesuit college. Although the girls' school was always referred to as 'Winckley Square', it was actually called The Holy Child Jesus Convent and School and it was run by a religious order called The Sisters of the Society of the Holy Child Jesus. It was an impressive red brick and stone edifice, with an imposing entrance portico. Our elder sister Veronica taught us how to sing the 'school song':

Come to Winckley, come to Winckley,
It's a place of misery.
There's a notice on the blackboard
Saying 'Welcome here to Thee'.
Build a bonfire, build a bonfire,
Put the textbooks on the top,
Put the teachers in the middle
And burn the rotten lot.

The third great Catholic stronghold in Preston was St Walburgh's Church. It was a huge Gothic church, as big as a cathedral. It boasted the tallest spire of any parish church in England. Just around the corner from Winckley Square, in Chapel Street, was the Catholic Church of St Wilfrid's. It was associated run by the Jesuits. In contrast to St Walburgh's, this was a church in the baroque renaissance style favoured by the Society of Jesus.

One of the reasons Dad overworked in the early days in Preston was that the modern languages teaching at Winckley Square, probably the German, was inadequate and so Dad was drafted in, presumably in his lunchtimes, free periods and after school, to cross the square and help out at the girls' school. This will have been Dad's first opportunity to teach girls and it may have influenced him to leave the security of his well-respected role at the College and move to a co-educational secondary modern school. Dad's nickname at Preston Catholic College was Big Ug, or just Ug. This apparently was a reference to his pronunciation of the German sound 'ach', which the boys themselves could not say properly.

Chapter 4

King's Drive, Fulwood

And a blue and white milk jug

In the garden there are two large, round circular flowerbeds. It is a bright, sunny afternoon. I am running around these flowerbeds laughing. There is another child running round in front of me. That is my sister, Bernadette. Mummy is chasing us, seriously trying to catch us. She wants us to come in for our afternoon sleep. We are at King's Drive. I am three years old. It is 1955. My mother and father have managed to buy their first family home. It is here that we will make our childhood memories.

King's Drive must have been developed between the wars. It linked Black Bull Lane with the Garstang Road. Some of the houses, like our friend Tom Kerr's, were very fine detached houses, with spacious, mature gardens, especially on the northern side of the road. Ours was a semi, but it was very well built, with rectangular bays running up the whole front of the house. Behind the bay was the lounge below and Mum and Dad's bedroom above. It had a front garden, fine brick gateposts with white square capping stones. From the gateposts hung double wooden gates in black and white. Contrary to Dad's rules, two of us would slot our feet between the upright bars at the centre of the gates and then push as hard as we could to see if we could beat each other to getting the gates fully open.

No 62 is the right-hand side of the semi, looking from the road. Next to the left-hand gatepost is a large yellow and green privet hedge which has been shaped as a bush. It is here one day that us boys play a dangerous game; to stand on the gate post and leap up and over the huge yellow privet bush and land six to eight feet below on the grass in the front garden. Edmund and Maurice can do it, but I don't dare. I decide to have a go on my own. I wait until there is no-one around. I stand and psych myself up for hours, until eventually I jump on my own with no-one looking or watching.

With Maurice at the front gates

King's Drive days. Mum and Dad are young and healthy and happy. Dad has a very good job at Preston Catholic College, where he is a very well-respected Head of Modern Languages. Money is tight, but not ridiculously so. We know we are not poor. We eat well. We have a 'Morning Room', kitted out with the most up-to-date furniture. There is a shiny black-topped dining room table, with flaps that fold down, and blue-grey legs that taper down to the metal studded feet. The legs can be screwed in and out and we do this whenever we want, without asking for permission. The legs can be used for naval guns, tank cannons or bazookas. The chairs are in stylish matching grey, with curved mid-century ply backrests. The seats are filled with a thin layer of foam and finished with plastic in a fetching yellow and black pattern. The dining set has a matching sideboard with a smart shiny black top surface made of Formica. On the left are three yellow drawers, to the right there are two levels, with sliding grey doors below and an upper compartment with sliding glass doors. Vertical gold lines run down the surface of the glass.

We eat from a wonderful Melamine tea set, with maroon saucers and grey cups. The grey cups gradually turn brown with tannin from the tea we drink. Our pottery milk jug is the epitome of modern design, in the form of a slanting parallelogram, white on the inside and Wedgwood blue on the outside.

King's Drive, pictured in 2022

Mum and Dad have achieved prosperity and respectability, a level domestic comfort. They are living proof of Macmillan's assertion of July 1957, that 'most of our people have never had it so good.'

You entered the house through a traditional door with large oval window in leaded glass. The front door was set in a covered but open porch. The step of the porch was made of a sort of pink stone. We said it looked like corned beef.

As you entered the hallway of the house, the lounge was on the left, with the door towards the further end of the room. On the right in the corner, in pride of place, was the television set. In the square bay window stood an elegant writing desk, with long Queen Anne legs. Matching the desk was a circular coffee table about 3' high and about 3' across. It had a carved wavy edge round the top. Underneath the top were housed four occasional tables with a quadrant profile. They rested on runners and could be slid out, to be placed next to armchairs so that guests could drink their tea. This did not happen often, because knick-knacks and ornaments sat on the lower deck of the little tables, just above the Queen Anne feet. The most intriguing object was the *Selcol* music box. This was a hexagonal structure made of wood, covered in black lacquer with delicate gold patterns. When you pressed the button on top the music started and the six doors opened, each with a curved compartment holding a stack of cigarettes. The doors were timed to open and close with the start and finish of the tune, a tune which every one of us would still be able to hum today, so often did we play with this box. The mechanism of the motor made a most luxurious sound when you wound it up by the key on the underneath. As the doors closed, they did so with a gentle click that was incredibly satisfying. Mum and Dad were both huge smokers, especially Mum. Her cigarette of preference was the modish Peter Stuyvesant, which came in a smart white packet with a red flash.

There was no settee. Instead, there were four armchairs in two pairs. The two main larger ones had big blocky straight flat upholstered arms, rounded at the front. The smaller ones had polished wooden arms which sloped up to an elegant curve. These had a detachable cushion, which sat on rows of long springs coated in black plastic. The pale blue material was quite hard and rough like a thick carpet. One of the smaller armchairs tended to live in the dining room in the corner by the French windows.

Nasturtiums would grow in a border that ran down the side of the garage. We were rather fascinated by the bright orange flowers and green textured leaves and snaking tubular stems. On the steps to the garden were two concrete octagonal urns with brick patters on the side. In these would grow geraniums. These two urns would one day be taken along to Bristol and then to Weston-Super-Mare.

If you walked out of the Morning Room, you came into a small bit of passage and turned right to arrive at the end of the hall. If you then went straight ahead you would go into the dining room, which had French windows which opened onto a large square sloping yard.

Straight across the corridor from the Morning Room was the door to a large understairs cupboard. In the floor of this cupboard was a hatch, which led into a large cellar-type space running underneath the length of the house. For some reason Dad did a job in the cellar which involved bricking up a wall. He ran a long rubber-coated extension wire all the way to where he was working. I climbed down and watched him working. I thought he must be incredibly brave and clever. He was happy and cheerful and waved. It was in this understairs cupboard that there sat for a long time a large bright red cylinder with a small screw cap opening at the top. This was the drum of Australian honey, another of Dad's madcap bargain purchases. It must have seemed like a good idea at the time, but the plan for a huge supply of cheap honey fell down on the question of how to access the contents of the drum. The honey was set and so it could not be poured out, but the small screw cap opening was the only way of getting to it. When we wanted some honey on our breakfast toast, we would take our knife to the understairs cupboard and poke around in the drum. Very soon it became impossible to get at any more of the honey and the entire drum had to be discarded after only a tiny fraction of its contents had been consumed.

I never felt poor when I lived in King's Drive, but I knew that we were not very well off, and the Australian honey incident only seemed to confirm that. I also realised that if we had been better off, we would not have had to go around in a car that was obviously an antique. When we needed a place to put our toys in our bedroom, Dad got hold of some wooden orange crates from the greengrocers. He screwed them together to make a nice cupboard with six compartments. He assembled all this outside on the sloping yard outside the French windows. He had no power tools and in order to drill holes through the wood he used a hand drill, with a nice polished wooden handle and a shiny orange cog wheel which turned the bit, I watched Dad work on the cupboard and played with his drill pretending it was a gun. Mum finished off our new toy cupboard with a curtain to go across the front and hide the contents. It was white cotton material with little coloured triangle shapes on it. Dad fixed it across the front with a sprung curtain wire.

Dad was always very skilful with his hands and while we were at Preston, he made us boys two wonderful items, a garage and a fire station. They were beautifully made of pine wood and ply, with proper ramps and metal windows. It is hard to imagine how Dad found the time to make these items.

Lytham St Anne's, which was not much more than an hour from where we lived. was a favourite seaside outing. Dad would drive past the main part of the town where the broad green lawns separated the road from the sea front. He would make his way to the farther, St Anne's end, and pull up on the side of the road by the sand dunes. There we would have a picnic. Then we would run up and down between the grassy hillocks. Lytham St Anne's was very clean and peaceful. When we got home to King's Drive, we would empty our shoes to see how much sand we had brought back.

It is a Sunday afternoon. Warm and sunny. Mum and Dad have decided to cut the hedges at the front of the house. They get the old brown army surplus blankets and spread them on the grass below the hedge in order to catch all the clippings. Dad is happy and is singing. He and Mum chat to each other. We mess about and play all around them, hindering, not helping. We have a beautiful home. There is a summer warmth in the air and a fresh scent of leaves and grass. I am at peace. I feel safe. I live at 62 King's Drive, Fulwood, Preston, Lancs.

Chapter 5

King's Drive Christmas

And Silent Night

At King's Drive Mum and Dad were able to create their first family Christmases. The season began on 5th December, on the evening of Dad's birthday. That night we would follow the German custom and put our shoes outside our bedroom doors so that we could wake up on St Nicholas' Day to find them filled with fruit and sweets. These were a reward for being good throughout the year. We knew that if we had been naughty, we would get a stick in our shoe, so that our parents could rap us with it as a punishment. We would question Mum again and again as to whether she had ever had a stick when she was little. She was wisely non-committal, knowing that this would only add to the mystique and tension of this special German tradition.

Before December, Omi would have sent over two or three Advent Calendars with nativity scenes and images on them. This was long before anyone in England had even heard of such a thing. We decorated the front room or lounge with salmon pink and white crêpe paper streamers. These were attached with Sellotape to the upside-down glass bowl lamp shade at the centre of the room. They were then sellotaped to the picture rail all round the room, creating what I considered to be a very magical effect, especially at night. After Christmas, these pink and white streamers were solemnly rolled up into tiny rolls and stored in a Quality Street tin. They got shorter and more dishevelled each year, as the Sellotape began to take its toll.

Mum and Dad worked so hard and were so busy that Christmas was a somewhat last-minute affair, with decorations only going up on Christmas Eve. The centrepiece of Christmas was the crib. This was made from a large, elegant, wickerwork baby crib, which had been used for each of the children in turn. This was then covered in black crêpe paper and the crib figures arranged inside. Some scrunched-up newspaper, or a trimmed-down cornflakes packet, was placed beneath the crêpe paper in order to create the effect of raised ground. Dad got an old tin can and cut a hole in the bottom of it.

He then got an old lamp fitting and fitted it to the bottom of the tin, with the flex coming out, and he then fitted the light bulb. It was at moments like this that Mum loved to come up to Dad and say something like 'Now Frank, are you sure that you have got that in the right place?' Dad would not say a word in response. He would leave his hands attached to whatever he was doing, turn his head slowly towards Mum, give her a glare with eyebrows raised, close his eyes, and sigh, and then resume his task. Dad used the open end of the tin to make a circle in some card, into which he could then cut a star shape. This was fixed to the tin with insulating tape and the light was then fixed on the top right-hand corner of the crib by pushing the wire through gap in the wickerwork. I loved Dad's ability to do things like this.

When I was asked at school to make a crib and bring it in, Dad helped me to fix a light in it with batteries and its own switch. I got an old piece of plywood and taped a shoe box onto it and then added lots of rolled up newspaper, all round the top and sides of the box. I then used papier-mâché to create a hillside cave effect. When the papier-mâché had dried, I painted it green and painted the inside of the shoe box black. Whenever we did papier-mâché projects at school the teacher would ask me to ask my mum for some flour. She never seemed to question this or to hesitate and would cheerfully furnish me with a large bag of flour, enough for the whole class.

In Germany it had been normal to put real candles on the Christmas tree, Mum had a set of clip-on candle holders and little candles which made the Christmas tree look marvellous. In those days there was no such thing as a Christmas tree in school or in a shop, and certainly not in church. On top of the tree was placed a Star of Bethlehem bauble which fitted over the top sprig of the tree and rose up in a silver spire. We thought it was very pagan to place a fairy on top of a Christmas tree.

Our crib figures were a much-loved set which lasted for many decades. They were made of very light plaster and were quite fragile, so that here and there you could see where Dad had glued and mended them. The angel wore a light blue tunic and knelt in prayer, with large wings outstretched. There was a very good ox and ass, both sitting down. Mary knelt in prayer, with her body and head turned towards the child Jesus. Joseph stood solemnly. The baby Jesus lay on fanned-out hay, with arms open in blessing.

The first king was an august and elderly figure, with white hair and beard and a long red cloak, which he held to one side with one hand. He stooped and bent forward as he approached the crib. The second king was more Mediterranean in appearance and the third king was black. He stood firmly and very self-confidently, with legs apart and a hand on his hip, and wore a turban on his head.

We would never have Christmas stockings and regarded with horror the idea of children getting up at the crack of dawn and tearing through their presents without their parents there. While Dad was creating the crib, putting up the tree and cursing the Christmas lights, Mum was busy ironing and collecting together our Sunday-best clothes. On Christmas morning it would be very cold and we would come down to the morning room, which had been heated by a two-bar plug-in electric fire. Each of us had a dining room chair on which all our washed and ironed clothes had been laid out neatly in little piles. We would then go off to St Anthony's for our Christmas morning Mass. At St Anthony's Church there was a magnificent crib. It was a work of art, entirely carved from one vast block of wood, almost certainly manufactured in Italy. It was about four or five feet in height and sat in front of the side chapel to the congregation's right. There were townsfolk and villagers all over the town and a network of alleyways and steps, all very tastefully finished in light pink and brown. After Mass, we would have a lovely German breakfast, with the usual *brötchen*, cheese and salami. On very special occasions like this, breakfast would begin with a luxurious glass of delicious grapefruit or pineapple juice from a large Del Monte tin.

After breakfast we would line up on the staircase from youngest to oldest and wait to hear noises from Father Christmas. We never seemed to use the expression Santa, which for some reason we thought was rather pagan. Dad would stomp round the room, grunting and groaning, which, when we were little, we found very frightening, even though deep down we probably knew that it was Dad. His acting out of Father Christmas' grumpy trudge round the room would reach a crescendo when the door suddenly exploded as if with gunfire. It was Dad hurling handfuls of nuts at the door. We would scream at the top of our voices. There would then be a bit of shuffling and murmuring and then a dramatic pause before Dad opened the door and let us in. 'Did you see him?' we would ask, as we stepped over the hazelnuts, walnuts, and almonds. But Dad would divert us by showing us the half-eaten carrot and mince pie and the half-drunk glass of sherry, sure signs that Father Christmas and his reindeer had visited.

We were still not allowed to fall upon our presents until we had gathered in front of the crib to sing *Stille Nacht*, Silent Night in German. Only then could we turn to our allocated armchair to open our presents.

Mum was bemused when she arrived in England and found that the English ate exactly the same thing at Christmas in three different forms, mince pies, Christmas cake and Christmas pudding. She did not make Christmas pudding, but her mince pies and Christmas cake were so good that we were spoiled; no subsequent mince pies or Christmas cake could ever live up to them. We had a stable home in a lovely area, with loving parents, wonderful food, and fascinating holiday adventures. Yet I grew up with the feeling of money worries nagging away at me, and an ill-defined feeling of impending financial disaster. Mum did not help in this respect, as she specialised in woe-is-me, doom-and-gloom scenarios. One year in December Mum announced that there would be no Christmas presents this year because Dad had no money. We all willingly said that it was not a problem and we would be quite happy to do without. Came the day, the Christmas presents would be there in abundance. But then the sight of them was still accompanied by the anxious thought that Dad could not really afford them. Without a doubt, paying for food, clothing, and schooling for six children on one teacher's salary in the leather elbow patched 1950s cannot have been easy, and that was the reality behind an ongoing, underlying sense of financial dread.

On the front steps at King's Drive

Chapter 6

St Anthony's Church

And a headful of candle wax

The Catholic community in Preston was very vibrant and was still growing in numbers in the post-war baby boom. For a long time, St Antony of Padua consisted of little more than a converted army hut. It was dingy and cramped and rather old and damp. Our family used to fill the front row on the right-hand side of the little church. However, while attending Mass in the hut we were able to witness the construction of a brand-new church, which was built on the land between the army hut and the main road, the Cadley Causeway. To get to St Anthony's you went down Black Bull Lane and turned right into Cadley Causeway. The foundation stone was laid in 1958. Before getting to the church, the Causeway passed over the railway track carrying the main line from Preston to Lancaster, Carlisle, and Scotland. Unknown to our parents, we would spend time on a Saturday hanging around on the railway line itself, placing copper coins on the line so that they would be defaced by passing trains. From the outside, the new St Antony's was simple but very imposing, with a very large tower. Inside, the nave had clear simple lines, in gentle curves and pure white walls. Once, as we came out of Mass in the old hut, the labourers were working high up in the roof area, fixing the timbers across the width of the nave of the new church. They were singing Catholic hymns at the top of their voices.

Although I did not know it then, the architect of our new church was the nationally acclaimed Giles Gilbert Scott, who was himself son of the even more famous George Gilbert Scott. The older, Victorian, Gilbert Scott was a Gothic revival architect, responsible for the Albert Memorial and St Pancras Station. The younger, St Antony's, Gilbert Scott was famous for the Liverpool Anglican Cathedral, as well as Battersea Power Station, the Cambridge University Library, and the iconic red British telephone boxes. Gilbert Scott died in 1960, just three months after the opening of the new St Antony's. The church is his last new church and remains unaltered from his original design.

We would often walk to church. One day, when we were walking to church, Dad pushed me in the middle of my back and told me to walk up straight and to stop slouching. He told me that his father had made him carry a stick behind his back with his arms passed over it so that he was forced to walk up straight and that he would do the same for me if I did not buck my ideas up.

St. Anthony's Church, pictured in 2022

On the day of my First Holy Communion Mum showed me the clothes I would wear. She had bought me a brand-new white shirt, smart light-grey shorts with creases down the front and back and with a shiny finish, a pair of new white socks and a beautiful shiny red bow tie. I was mightily impressed by these clothes and pestered Mum to let me wear them. The Holy Communion ceremony was not until the afternoon and I would not give in until she had let me put them on. Once I had them on, I got bored and asked Mum if I could go for a ride round the block. Again, Mum was extremely reluctant, but gave in once again, telling me how expensive the clothes were and how I had to make sure that I did not get them dirty. I went off for my ride and of course I somehow managed not only to crash and fall off my bike, but even made sure that I tumbled off into a huge muddy puddle. Soon I was knocking on the kitchen door and Mum came out to see me sobbing and dripping with mud. She should have shouted and screamed at me after all the care and the money she had spent on preparing me to look my best for my First Holy Communion, but she did not. She calmly got me changed and by the time we set off for church I was undeservedly kitted out in a perfectly washed and ironed outfit.

The only thing I can remember from my First Holy Communion was that we had to line up in one of the classrooms before heading over to the church and a grim and grumpy nun spent the whole time scowling at us and shushing us up and poking us in our backs, which was all completely unnecessary as we were all queuing in a silent and orderly fashion, too terrified to move a muscle. The reception of the host was nerve-wracking, but went very smoothly. Miss Brown had trained us for hours in the classroom, using a knitting needle. We would kneel down in front of her desk, place out tongues right out and Miss Brown would place her knitting needle on our tongues. As soon as we felt the knitting needle, we were to retract our tongue neatly. We were then to pretend to swallow the host without biting it in any way. On the day itself it was very intimidating because we had to go up to the altar rails in full view of the congregation, then wait our turn to kneel at the altar rail, then wait for the altar boy to place the patten under our chin, while the priest spoke the words, *Corpus Christi*.

From then on, I would join my older brothers and sisters in going to Confession regularly on a Saturday afternoon. We would do the half hour walk together down to St Anthony's, while Mum and Dad stayed at home. There would be several pews worth of penitents waiting patiently alongside the confessional boxes, and the whole process would take a couple of hours out of our Saturday.

Upon our return we were rewarded with a drink of squash and a Lyons chocolate marshmallow teacake covered in silver paper. Another two hours were lost on a Sunday afternoon, attending or serving Benediction. Apart from the blessing of the congregation, with the monstrance held in the cloth of the cope, the highlight of this service was the echoing of the Divine Praises, starting with *Blessed be God*, and the chanting of the *Tantum Ergo*.

On one occasion we were all at Sunday Mass at St Anthony's, seated half way up the nave on the right-hand side. Just before Communion I turned to my older sister Veronica and told her that I did not think that I could receive communion as I thought I had done something wrong. Veronica told me not to worry about it, but at the Elevation of the Host, to bring my worry to Jesus and this would be enough to prepare me to receive Holy Communion. Veronica was a very wise older sister to whom I could always turn for advice.

At Corpus Christi there would be an annual Corpus Christi procession, in which the Blessed Sacrament, in the parish's finest monstrance, would be borne through the streets surrounding the church, with an embroidered canopy held above and the priest dressed as for Benediction, in full ornamental cope. All altar servers were needed for this occasion, to hold the four supporting poles of the embroidered canopy, to precede the procession creating clouds of incense with the thurible, or to walk in twos in front. The whole parish followed behind singing *Sweet Sacrament Divine* and other eucharistic hymns. I remember looking at the pavements and seeing passers-by going about their everyday business. Their reaction to the procession was not one of hostility, but of mere indifference, or sheer incomprehension. I felt very sorry for them, that they had to live their lives outside the community of faith.

Once we had done our First Holy Communion, Maurice and I immediately joined the altar servers' rota. There was a weekday 7am Mass which had to be served, wearing black cassocks rather than the Sunday red. For one week in every month, at the ages of eight or nine, we would get ourselves up at 6.30am and walk down to church on our own to serve the early morning Mass. This was not a punishment or a chore. We did not expect or receive any praise or even encouragement for doing it. It was a privilege and we enjoyed taking full responsibility for getting ourselves up and dressed and down to the church, which was a mile and a half walk each way, in time to get changed and serve the Latin Mass.

The Parish Priest, Canon Geoghan, was a kindly but elderly priest with considerable power and authority over the community. He regularly came to King's Drive to share our Sunday tea with us. Rather than sit at the table he would sit on one of the light armchairs just near the French windows, while we all sat round the table. He would have a cup of tea and a few bits to eat on a plate on his lap. He was extremely fond of Mum and Dad and lent them money for the holiday in Scotland.

Fr Bootle was regarded as a bit of a joke. He had round NHS 'Captain Pocket' spectacles and a fussy nervous manner. In one of his homilies, he once said 'St Bernadette was ordinary girl, just like you and me.' Dad thought this was hilarious and quoted it endlessly. Once at a very long service Maurice fainted, and I also think that on another occasion either Maurice or I was sick and threw up on the altar rails. One of the servers went to the sacristy and got a cardboard box to put over the vomit while the service continued. I am pretty sure it did not matter too much because it was Benediction rather than Sunday Mass. I once had to serve Stations of the Cross, which meant being one of the two acolytes or candle-bearers to walk and stand on either side of the priest as he made his way round the fourteen stations. The brass candlestick was too heavy for me and I kept holding it at an angle. This meant that wax was dripping continuously onto my head for the whole hour of the service. When the service finished and I went home the whole crown of my head was a huge dome of set wax, looking just like a monk's tonsure. Neither of my parents worried or commented on any aspect of this.

My favourite priest was Fr Boyle. He was a young priest with fair hair. He was quite large and even a bit overweight. He knew how to talk to the altar boys and always made a point of thanking us, or of explaining exactly how to do our jobs. He enjoyed laughing and joking and made sure we behaved ourselves but also that we enjoyed our serving. For Bonfire Night one year Fr Boyle organised for a huge bonfire to be built on the waste land between St Anthony's and the railway line. He organised for every altar boy to go home and ask our mums to provide an old sock stuffed full with other socks. Mum duly obliged and I was very proud to give Fr Boyle my stuffed sock. The purpose of the socks was to act as firelighters. The bonfire had got very wet with Lancashire rain during the end of October and beginning of November.

On the actual night we all gathered round the bonfire and Fr Boyle got a jerry can and poured petrol into a bucket and then soaked the sock firelighters in petrol. He then placed them all round the bonfire and tossed matches in until there was an almighty woosh of fire and flames. We loved it because we had helped to build the bonfire with old bits of wood and had helped to light it. We were allowed to dance and run around and mess about as much as we liked. Not a single thought was given to health and safety.

A few years after my First Holy Communion, I was able to celebrate my Confirmation, a much more impressive affair. I was confirmed by Bishop Pearson, the Bishop of Lancaster. He was an august and imposing man, but very spiritual and not at all intimidating or pompous. The confirmation did not take place in our church of St Anthony's, but at St Edward's. The full name of this church was Our Lady and St Edward's. It was not far from us. You had to go north up the Garstang Road and it was off to the left in a road called Lightfoot Lane. The design of this church was not dissimilar to St Anthony's, with a brown brick exterior and simple white-painted walls inside. But it was bigger, and on the occasion of the confirmation it was packed with children and their families from all over the area. We sang *Come Holy Ghost Creator Come* at the top of our voices, and at Communion, *Soul of my Saviour*. Bishop Pearson took time to look each of us in the eyes and to administer the sacrament in a caring and respectful way, even though he did not know any of us. I felt very inspired by the grandeur, the simplicity and the seriousness of the occasion and cherished this day inside me for the rest of my life.

Once St Anthony's Church was built, with its lovely semi-circular arches and its fine *baldachino* over the altar, the parish decided to construct a new school building. All the children of the parish were issued with little collecting cards with a diagram of a pyramid of bricks inside. Each brick cost a sixpence and we were to shade in a brick every time we sold a brick and got sixpence. Maurice and I went all along Westgate and Regent's Drive together and knocked on every door, asking people if they would like to buy a brick to build a new Catholic Primary School of St Anthony of Padua. Almost everybody was happy to oblige and buy a brick. On Saturdays the dads of the parish would go down to church and help to build the new school.

We went down one Saturday and watched the professional brickies building the wall, while Dad with some other dads wheel-barrowed loads of soil and sand and cement and bricks. I was immensely proud to see Dad helping to build the school.

For the annual altar boys' outing we went to Blackpool. The priests hired our transport from the cheapest firm available and so an ancient antique bus rolled up outside St Anthony's to take us there. The engine stuck out in front of the split screen windscreen. The seats were upholstered with dark green cracked leather, with curved tops and chrome fittings. When we got to Blackpool, we had to spend hours trudging through the so-called pleasure grounds. A lot of the boys seemed to understand Blackpool and know what to do. They bought cowboy hats and huge sticks of candy floss. The highlight of the visit was the circus in the arena at the bottom of the Blackpool Tower. We had very good seats and Fr Boyle, who had organised the trip and was in charge, sat among us, beaming with pleasure and happiness. He laughed at all the clowns and loved every act and every animal. I thought it was rather squalid and came back home with a headache. This was not helped by the huge animated statue of a man, situated at the entrance to the pleasure grounds, emanating nightmarish laughter on a permanent loop. This brought on a panic attack in me, as there was no escape from the endless repetition. I made a firm resolution never to go on the altar boys' trip again.

Chapter 7

St Vincent's School

And a bouquet of lilac

W e three boys did not go to St Anthony's School but to St Vincent's. Apart from St Vincent's Road, which still leads off the east side of the Garstang Road, there is no evidence of the vast Victorian edifice that was St Vincent's School and Orphanage for Boys. The building housed both a normal primary school and a sort of middle school where the older orphan boys were taught practical subjects like woodwork and metal work. The most impressive thing about St Vincent's was the enormous ornamental tower built like the rest of the orphanage in red brick and rising high above the covered entrance porch. The orphanage had been built on a 17-acre site and opened in 1896. At its height it had capacity for 300 boys.

My first teacher at St Vincent's was the fearsome and crabby Miss Brown. She used to cycle into school through the front door and turn right along the main corridor, past the office of the headmaster Mr Dobbin. She would then turn right again and sail straight into our classroom, to park her traditional sit-up-and-beg bicycle on the right between the door and the Nature Table.

The classroom was vast and must have been designed to hold two years' worth of pupils, Reception and Year 1. If you misbehaved you had to come up to Mrs Brown's ancient high traditional desk with integral seat. You stood in front of the desk and placed your hands over the front edge of the desk, which was high above your head. She would then rap your knuckles with a dark brown wooden dowelling rod about the length of a ruler.

When I first started at St Vincent's I got completely confused about the timing of the school day. At the end of the day, I went up the steps to the refectory to have my lunch. The double doors were locked and I banged on them, crying my eyes out and wondering why they would not let me in to have my lunch. When someone came to tell me to go home because school was over, I could not believe them and had no memory of having my lunch.

I had to trudge my way home alone, and found out that this could be a perilous business. We would make our way with trepidation along the unmade St Vincent's Road, passing the Carmelite Convent on our left. Occasionally we would go to the Carmelite Convent for Mass. This was a most mysterious experience, as we could hear the nuns chanting and responding to the prayers, but could not see them beyond a black portcullis-style grille. The Convent did not close until 2023. Just as the road met the Garstang Road there was a high bank on the right with tall trees on it. The Protestants used to wait up on the bank on the right behind the trees and then ambush us by hurling rocks and stones and verbal abuse. We would never retaliate against these assaults by the 'Proddy-Dogs'. I would like to say that this was because it had been drummed into us that it would be wrong. I suspect it was because we knew we would be thoroughly beaten. We simply kept our heads down and made a dash for it, knowing that the Garstang Road would be too public for the attack to continue.

St Vincent's was very primitive. The yard was surrounded by a high brick wall, just like a prison yard. This must have been designed to keep the orphans in. The boys' urinal was a section of this wall covered in black waterproofing tar, with a simple brick screen wall in front. The older boys never used it in a straightforward way. Instead. they tried to outdo each other in how high up the wall their urine could reach. If the splashes fell down all over us younger boys, then this only added to their amusement. The brick wall was also useful for playing cigarette cards. Every boy at this time would have a collection of cigarette packets, picked up from the street or from parents. The aim was to have as large and varied a collection as possible. You won another boy's card by throwing them together and getting closer to the wall. Maurice and I were both very keen on Craven A, as these bright red square packets were very smart and most prestigious, but also because they flew very well. Others we liked to have in our collection were Du Maurier, Strand, Pall Mall, Embassy, Players, and Park Drive.

The Nature Table was the only thing of interest in the classroom, the one thing we could feel ownership of. Anyone could bring things in and place them on the table, favourites being birds' nests, birds' eggs, pine cones and Autumn leaves. After a year the crabby Miss Brown seemed to disappear, to be replaced by her polar opposite, Miss Helm. Miss Helm was young. She was a very intelligent and skilful teacher. She loved children. She smiled, not just with her mouth but with her eyes. She was tall and slim. She had perfect skin and beautiful black wavy hair, cut off in a sort of messy bob.

One day Miss Helm told us that we were going on an adventure. It was going to be a picnic. Not a whole school trip, but a special little trip just for our class. Not a whole day, just an afternoon. For that day we were to organise a picnic for ourselves in a suitable bag or container and we must make sure to bring a drink. There would be no need for a bus or coach journey. We would walk to the picnic! Just our class. Us and Miss Helm.

The day came and turned into a beautiful sunny afternoon. Everyone was perfectly behaved and followed Miss Helm in pairs along the little path that led to the golf links behind St Vincent's School. We soon turned right down a lane and then turned left off the lane into the grounds of the golf club. A beautiful bright clear stream, which Miss Helm called the Savick Brook, meandered its way through the grassy slopes of the golf course. Miss Helm found a lovely area right next to the stream and we all sat down quietly to enjoy our picnic. This was a time before Tupperware and drinks bottles. The sandwiches that we unwrapped came out of brown paper, bread wrappings or greaseproof paper, all tied up with string or ribbon. Drinks were in Thermos flasks, or recycled NHS orange juice bottles. One girl sitting next to me had been given her drink in a dark blue Milk of Magnesia bottle. The drinks were water, milk, Ribena, or orange squash. I said to Miss Helm, 'Look, that girl is drinking out of an ink bottle,' but Miss Helm told me not to be silly. She did not organise us in any way or try to make us play any games. Instead, she let us sit quietly, chatting together, and then let us take off our shoes and socks to paddle in the stream, chasing tiddlers in the water and filling our bottles and emptying them. She sat calmly on the green grass with her knees drawn up and her hands joined round them. When it was time to go, the picnic had not been too long and it had not been too hurried. It had been just right. Time had been suspended. We had had a little taste of heaven.

Around this time, I had a dream about Miss Helm. For several years this dream would recur. It would be the same each time. I would be standing at the bottom of a long flight of stairs, with white-painted woodwork. Miss Helm would appear at the top of the stairs. She would be wearing a Christian Dior New Look dress. The dress was made of shiny stain. The sleeves came down and stopped at the elbow. The colour of the dress was violet. Miss Helm would place a white gloved hand on the banister on her right-hand side and my left.

She would pause for a moment and would then skip lightly down the stairs in her white high-heel shoes with pointed shoes. She never quite reached the bottom. Her black shiny hair would bob as she came down smiling and laughing, with her mouth slightly open with bright red lipstick.

Many years later I was walking down the main corridor at St Brendan's, when one of the teachers, Porky Patten, stopped me and said, 'Mohan, I bumped into an old friend of yours this weekend at a conference. I don't know if you remember her, a Miss Helm. She asked how you were getting on and sends you her regards.'

The most beautiful girl in the class was Katherine MacFarlane. She was also the most intelligent pupil and endured her education with an air of detachment. She was a brunette, with a fine head of luxurious Celtic hair. It was usually held back in a well-organised pony tail. One day she and I were chosen to act out a drama in front of the class. We stood near the Nature Table. We enjoyed making the words up on the spot, working together and performing to the whole class. We never spoke to each other before or after this incident.

As we got older, all three of us boys were taught by Miss Baldwin and all of us remember her very well. She was a first-class teacher whom I greatly admired. She truly loved her pupils and was extremely ambitious for their success and happiness in their future lives. Miss Baldwin had such a powerful aura that she seemed like a creature from another world, from a film perhaps. Handsome was a word that could be used to describe her. She had jet black hair, parted precisely in the centre, drawn down on either side and gathered up into an extremely neat bun at the back. Her face was very pale, her eyes large, bright, and intelligent. She wore the same thing every day. A short black cardigan, gathered in at the waist and a long, full, black, pleated skirt. She had black polished shoes and dark stockings with a line down the back. Miss Baldwin's desk was in the right-hand corner as you faced the glazed partition wall between her classroom and Miss Brown's. She was usually seated at her tall beechwood desk, or standing just next to it. Next to her desk was a high windowsill on which stood a huge brown glass jar with a metal screw top lid. The jar contained hundreds of tiny milk sweets. They were just like vitamin tablets or pills, light brown and tasting of malted milk. These were handed out as rewards for good work or good behaviour. One of the high points of Miss Baldwin's life had been a visit to Rome. This lent her an exotic air. 'You can fry an egg on the pavement in Rome,' was an oft-stated piece of information she shared with us, with a wistful tone in her voice.

Miss Baldwin explained to us that the English were savages who had not the first idea about cooking and that the Italians understood that one should always cook with olive oil and not with ghastly animal fat. She also told us that one day they would invent telephones which would have screens, on which callers would be able to see each other. 'I am not at all sure that I would like people to see me in my dressing gown' she said. This was all very interesting, partly because at that time we had not even seen a telephone, but also because we were not at all sure what to make of the thought of Miss Baldwin in a dressing gown.

When we made our First Holy Communion, a lavish buffet of party food was set out on the classroom desks in Miss Baldwin's room. The desks were put together and covered with table cloths and a magnificent spread laid out. I have no idea how or why I came to be in the room on my own, but as usual I was in the wrong place at the wrong time. As I stood there, a menacing posse of oversized orphans came bursting in from the door to Mis Brown's class, shaking the glazed partition as they slammed the door closed. 'Is this food for us?' they asked me, exchanging knowing grins and towering over me. I managed to say a lily-livered 'Well, yes, I suppose it could be', before making a dash for the door and out into the yard. When it came to the actual First Holy Communion meal, there were significant amounts of food missing. The next day, as Miss Baldwin was teaching us, the classroom door flew open and in stormed a furious Mr Dobbin, the Headteacher, holding an ugly-looking orphan by the ear. 'Well, which one is it?' he shouted at the wretch. Sure enough, the orphan food-thief pointed at me. 'It were 'im.' I was not beaten by Mr Dobbin, but I was shouted at and berated with endless cries of 'How dare you!' and 'What a disgrace you are!' and 'Just wait until your parents hear about this' and 'Our First Holy Communion feast completely ruined' and 'You would think he would have more sense.' I thought it was Mr Dobbin who should have more sense. This was one of those moments when I lost respect for adults and realised what fools they can be.

I felt the same way later when something happened to me in that same classroom. Miss Baldwin decided to go round the class and ask us what we would like to be when we grow up. When it came to my turn, I said 'Bus conductor.' I was not trying to be facetious. The buses from Preston used to use the crossroads with Black Bull Lane and King's Drive, what we called 'The Corner', as a sort of terminal. They would park up for a while before returning to town down Black Bull Lane to the Plungington Road.

Their parking bay was at the top of Boys Lane, where there was a wide expanse of pavement. We used to hang around there and chat to the bus conductors. They were a very friendly bunch and they seemed to have the best job in the world. They were care-free and happy as they stood on the platform and whistled, or ran up and down the stairs, or, best of all, turned the dial on the top of their steel ticket machine and issued a ticket with a turn on the handle with one hand and the tearing off of the ticket with the other hand. Miss Baldwin was apoplectic. She had never heard such a shocking answer in all her life. I was made to stand on my chair, while Mr Dobbin, the foolish headmaster, was summoned from his office next to the tower. When he arrived, he had to take his lead from Miss Baldwin, of whom he was terrified, and came out with a string of 'Well, what a disappointment,' and 'I cannot believe what I am hearing.' I was exhaustively interrogated as to the reasons for my answer, while still standing on my chair in full view of the entire class, who were all enjoying not being the one in trouble. I was disgusted that they could be so disrespectful of the worthy vocation of the bus conductor.

On the side of the buses in Preston was the town's symbol or coat of arms. It consisted of a seated Lamb of God with a halo round his head and bearing the cross from which flew a pennant as sign of the Risen Lord. I used to see this emblem and think how wonderful it was that even the buses were Catholic.

Once I was coming back from the direction of town on a bus. I had probably just been for a haircut. I decided it would look very cool if, instead of waiting for the bus to stop, near Mr Wybrow's grocery store, I would calmly step off early, while the bus was moving. I wanted to look like a very successful businessman who was so busy and important that he did not need to wait for the bus to stop. I stepped off far too early while the bus was still going far too fast. The momentum made me fall and roll over, smashing right into a lamppost and nearly knocking myself out. I did not tell my parents anything about this incident. As a general policy, I tried never to tell my parents anything and lived in my own private world.

I had a further humiliation when reading out loud in Miss Baldwin's class. In the afternoons, at reading time, we would take it in turns to read out loud. We were reading from a Geography book and I had to read the word Russia. I pronounced it phonetically, as Russ-ia, and did not even realise that I was making a mistake.

Miss Baldwin was livid because she presumed that I was doing this deliberately. Perhaps she was wary of me after the bus conductor incident. She made fun of my pronunciation and the whole class laughed at me. I was mortified.

Another incident from Miss Baldwin's classroom was not my fault. We were doing singing, which meant that some old-fashioned benches, with metal fold down rickety legs, were brought to the front and we were seated, six or eight to a bench, in two rows. I was on the back row and we were waiting for the session to start. Some boys got bored and decided it would be fun to put their feet on the bench in front and try to rock it to and fro. All they did was rock our own bench, which eventually fell right over backwards, with all the children falling in a heap. I instinctively put my hands on the back edge of the bench and these got crushed between the bench and the floor with the weight of the children on top of my hands. When we had all got back up, I was crying and in a state of shock. My hands were shaking and eight of my fingers completely crushed. For the perpetrators no form of punishment was issued and no form of medical attention was provided for me. I was not able to use my hands at all for a week or so, but fortunately nothing was broken. The singing lesson had proceeded as normal. We had to sing '*Old Macdonald had a farm ..*'. I had always rather disliked this song, as I thought it banal and repetitive, but from then on, I truly loathed it. Music consisted of singing folk songs like this. Songs I enjoyed included '*Do you ken John Peel*', '*Bobby Shafto*', '*Mairi's Wedding*' and '*Over the sea to Skye*'.

Above Miss Baldwin's classroom was a vast hall or room which extended over the area of both Miss Brown's and Miss Baldwin's rooms. This was a gymnasium with a fine timber sprung floor. If it was too wet outside for us to play in the prison yard, we would have our break in this room. This was quite good fun because the room was equipped with medicine balls of various sizes and we could spend our time lifting them and trying to hurl them at each other.

After Miss Baldwin's I graduated to Mr McManaman's class. To get to his class you carried on along the dark corridor past the entrance to Miss Brown's and Miss Baldwin's and turned right into a much smaller classroom. You had to be careful not to continue to the end of the corridor, for here there was a door to the orphanage and behind this door lay a woodwork workshop. Barry McManaman was a young, rather dashing teacher, who no doubt regarded Miss Brown and Miss Baldwin as dinosaurs. He was more friendly and seemed to like teaching and to like children. He would take his jacket off and teach in his white shirt and shiny suit trousers.

I was already useless at sport. One day Mr McManaman taught us all how to play cricket, which he really loved. I did enjoy this lesson and liked the leisurely rhythms and rituals of the game. At the end of the afternoon, he walked with us back from the field to the school. As we were walking along, he suddenly shouted 'Catch!' and hurled a cricket ball at me from a distance of about ten feet. I was so inept I did not really cotton on to what was happening until it was too late. The bright red leather crashed into my nose, nearly breaking it, and leaving me with terrible bruising and scabs for days. Poor Mr McMenaman was mortified, but he had every right to expect a young lad to enjoy catching a ball that was thrown to him.

His classroom was a rather dingy affair. In May he asked us to bring flowers in and he would place them in vases round the statue of Our Lady, which was on a shelf high up on the right-hand side near the door to the classroom. I went home and asked Mum if I could take some lilac in to put round the statue of Our Lady. Mum cut me down several huge branches of lilac in perfect bloom and I took them in. Mr McManaman and I put them in vases before the class started. I had happily walked all the way from home to school with the vast bunch of lilac. When we said our morning prayers Mr McManaman pointed out the lilac and told the class that I had brought it in. All week the whole room was filled with the scent of lilac. I would look at it and think of our garden at home.

Chapter 8

The Corner

And Mrs Corbett's

I did not really know the centre of Preston at all. My little world was lived out in the confines of Fulwood, with Black Bull Lane to the west, and the Garstang Road to the east. In between these two main thoroughfares were the tranquil, almost traffic-free, suburban streets where our cycling took place; Westgate, Southgate and Eastgate. We also made use of Regent's Drive, which ran parallel to King's Drive to the south. Like King's Drive, it linked the Garstang Road to Black Bull Lane. To get a haircut, us three boys would have to walk down Black Bull Lane and over the crossroads onto the Plungington Road, which did what it said by plunging straight on all the way into town. The barber's was on the right in the front room of a red-brick terraced house. The hairdresser was a bad-tempered brute who enjoyed tugging viciously at our hair with his nasty blunt scissors. Fringes were cut in a straight diagonal, down from the parting and across the forehead. The theory was that this allowed you to Brylcreme your hair back and up over to the side. The reality was that for years our hair sat flat on our foreheads in a bizarre diagonal line. While my hair was being cut, I would look at a display card called Durex. It was faded pink and blue in colour. An attractive blonde stretched her face up and arched her neck and looked me straight in the eye, with lips parted to reveal perfect white teeth.

The Corner was a very important place which we knew intimately. It was a very large crossroads, where King's Drive at its west end met Black Bull Lane. If you turned right as you arrived at the Corner, there was a very broad pavement and two or three shops, the last and most important of which was Mrs Corbett's, the newsagent and sweet shop. We were allowed to go to the Corner as often as we wanted and whenever we wanted. Every Saturday we would go to spend our pocket money on sweets and comics. This depended on whether Dad had issued us with our weekly wage. We would stand around his chair after Saturday morning breakfast and look at him in anticipation, until either he or one of us brought up the topic of pocket money. Sometimes he would say that he could not afford to give us our pocket money. This was the cue for Edmund to reach for his account book, where he kept a record of Dad's debts.

Maurice and I were the very best of friends throughout our childhood and adolescence. We could not afford individually to buy both the Victor and the Beano every week so we formed a cooperative, pooling our resources and purchasing one copy of each to share. The Victor started in January 1961, so it was not regarded as old-fashioned at all, but as a very exciting new arrival on the comic scene. We were brought up in the lea of the Second World War, with the war forming a continuous backdrop to our lives, our games, our reading, and our identity. The flagship story each week in the Victor, which gave the magazine its name, was the tale of a member of the armed

Maurice

forces who had been awarded the VC. This would be the cover story and would continue in colour on the back page. Our favourite feature inside the magazine was *Alf Tupper – Tough on the Track*. The plot was the same each week. Alf had to juggle attendance at his running events with his work commitments as a welder. The thought bubbles would tell us what Alf was thinking, such 'I ain't goin' to get this done on time.' Alf was a loner and a working-class hero, who had to compete with pampered semi-professional athletes who belonged to sports clubs, wore smart club blazers, and only ate the finest food. Alf was short in stature, with a rugged, honest face, which often sported a one- or two-day stubble. The middle-class athletes tended to have floppy blond hair, long sharp noses, and smooth features with smirking snooty expressions. Each week Alf would overcome some sort of new adversity, usually hurling himself over the line at the very last moment.

In the army stories, the British soldiers had friendly, but gritty, cockney faces. The ordinary Tommy tended to wear his helmet at a jaunty angle, while the officers were invariably tall, dark, and handsome. German troops had faces which followed the profile of their helmets, with huge square jaws. They were regularly drawn with staring, terrified eyes and mouths open in a scream or a snarl, as they fielded the gallant British attack. As popular as Alf Tupper, and in the same vein as the cover VC story was the feature on a Second World War pilot by the name of Matt Braddock. More exotic and lots of fun was Morgyn the Mighty, a strong man on a desert island called Black Island.

If you crossed over the road opposite Mrs Corbett's there was a similarly wide pavement and a corresponding parade of shops. The one on the corner of Boys Lane belonged to the Wybrows and their grocery store. As you came in on the left there was a large array of square glass-topped biscuit boxes, from which you could make up your own assortment, including broken biscuits. Wybrows had a better selection of chocolate than Mrs Corbett, who tended to specialise in traditional sweets in sweet jars, including Edmund's famous Pear Drops. We had to go to Wybrows for McCowan's Highland Toffee, Caramac, Spangles and Love Hearts.

On one dramatic morning we arrived at the Corner to see a fire engine pulled up on the broad pavement and smoke billowing out of the windows above the store. It turned out that Wybrow's only son Brent had set fire to his bed. Forever after we would call a fire engine Brent's Burnt Bed Brigade and would challenge each other to repeat it at high speed. We regarded Mr Wybrow as something of a wide boy, with his crew cut and all-American approach to life, while Brent we regarded as a spoilt brat.

Just along from the Wybrows was a greengrocers. Mum once sent me there with instructions to return with a cucumber. When I asked for a cucumber, the lady said 'Now hang on a minute, you can't possibly want a whole cucumber.' The lady behind me in the queue chipped in and said 'Oh yes he will. I know this boy and he's from a very large family.' The last few words were mouthed *sotto voce*, accompanied by the exchange of a knowing look. On one occasion Dad took us to Blackpool and we were all walking along the Promenade. A well-meaning middle-class lady sidled up to Mum and Dad and said 'Excuse me sir, I just want to say how marvellous I think it is that you should be giving these orphans a day out.'

Mum prided herself on keeping on good terms with next door neighbours. In King's Drive this meant Molly and Peggy on one side, and Mrs Bilsborrow on the other. Mum would also visit Mrs Walmsley in Regent's Drive. Regent's Drive was a cut above and Mrs Walmsley was definitely from the top drawer. Mum once took me there for afternoon tea. Mrs Walmsley was an elderly woman with a very kindly disposition and the very fine speaking voice of an actress. Having been warned by Mum to be on best behaviour, I was extremely polite and courteous. This perhaps paid off for me, because when we moved to Bristol, Mrs Walmsley gave Mum her piano. It was an upright piano, but it was cross-strung, which meant that it could achieve the richness and power of a baby grand. It had been built between the wars and was housed in a magnificent mahogany case which folded forward over the keyboard to create a huge rectangular box.

Mum was also very good at making friends and connecting with people. An example of her open attitude to all was her welcoming of the local window cleaners. These would come and do the street in groups of three or four workers. They would bring white enamel billy-cans with them, which their wives had already filled with tea leaves. When the time came for their elevenses, they would come from all over the street and gather on the corned-beef doorstep of our front porch. Mum would then boil the hot water and fill their cans with tea. They were always chatting and laughing together. In order to get a nice strong brew, they would stand up and hold the billy-can by the carrying handle and swing it round in the air in a great big circle. I thought we were very privileged that our house was chosen as the gathering place of these impressive men.

On Friday nights Mum used to do the ironing. She loved this time and would put on the radio and listen to *Sing Something Simple* on the Light Programme, with Cliff Adams and the Cliff Adams Singers. This programme would create a happy, peaceful atmosphere in the house. It started with its theme song:

Sing Something Simple,
As cares go by,
Sing Something Simple,
Just you and I.

A voice would then come on and say 'We invite you to sing something simple and join in with all the songs you know so well.'

Mum taught me how to iron a shirt. You start with the collar, which you never iron along its length, but up and down across the collar's width, to avoid any nasty creases. You then place the buttoned side panel face down on the ironing board, using the point of the iron to work carefully around the buttons, then the other panel. Now the back and shoulder panel, and finish with the cuffs, face down and ironed like the collar up and down, not across the length. She also taught me how to fold the shirt by buttoning it up, placing it face down, folding in one side to within two inches of the collar, then folding the arm back down the length of the die, then the same with the other side and sleeve. Three folds, starting at the bottom end, would then create a neat rectangle which would fit in a drawer. It has given me great pleasure to use this system for over sixty years. Mum also taught me to sew, how to choose the right needle and cotton, how to lick the cotton end and thread the needle, how to knot it at one end then trim off any excess, and how to create the knot at the end of the task using the needle in the right hand and the nail of the left hand. One of her rules was never to try to use too long a thread. She used to say to me, 'Francis, even the best sewer in the world would not be able to sew with a thread of that length.' She made me sew on shirt buttons, which was a very useful skill, encouraging me to be self-reliant.

One person we nearly caused Mum to fall out with was the cleaner who came to help her out with the household chores. The cleaner was mopping the hall one day and told us children to 'Mind the bookit.' 'It's bucket, not bookit,' we said to the cleaner, presuming she might appreciate some help with her elocution. She downed tools and stormed off to find Mum. 'Well, aw've never bin saw insulted in all ma life,' she shouted at Mum. Mum did not really tell us off very much, but treated us to a full account of the crisis and how she had used her diplomatic skills to secure the cleaner's continued services.

As Black Bull Lane passed down towards town, it crossed over a small bridge which was built over the stream, the Savick Brook, that ran through the golf course. One year there were exceptionally heavy rains which caused the brook to burst its banks and the bridge had to be closed to traffic. We all walked down in the darkness and stood looking down into the stream, which had become a treacherous, violent torrent. A man standing next to Dad said 'You know I wouldn't be able to swim across that, and I'm a strong swimmer.' For some reason we found this funny and would repeat it endlessly afterwards.

One of our happy places in Fulwood was the Fulwood Library. This was within easy walking distance. You had to cross the Garstang Road and make your way a mile or so, passing Black Bull Lane on your left and carrying on for a few hundred yards. Fulwood Library was set back from the Garstang Road with an expanse of green grass in front. A low brick wall formed its boundary at the pavement. We loved this wall because we could climb up onto it and run along the top before turning right into the library. It was capped with broad stones, which made it very easy to walk along. After a few yards the wall went down a level by means of a curved section of stone coping, which you could run down. We all had library tickets and would visit the library very often on a Saturday. The little library building was made of brick and had a sort of art deco curved entrance lobby at the front. When I was little, I got out all the Rev Awdry's Thomas the Tank engine books in turn. Later Maurice and I worked our way through all Richmal Crompton's *William* books, before moving on to *Jennings*, which both Maurice and I loved. Jennings and his best friend Derbyshire were at a boarding school. They would be allowed to go into the local village, where there was a shop called '*Chas. Lumley. Home-Made Cakes. Bicycles Repaired.*' We were especially fond of Mr Carter, the House Master who was so understanding of all the confusions and foibles of the boys in his care.

On the way to the library, we would walk past the Harris Orphanage, which was on the King's Drive side of the Garstang Road. This vast Victorian estate always held an air of mystery. We would walk past with a sense of awe. From the road it looked a bit like a monastery or a convent. The buildings were quite low lying and there was a huge church-like spire, very similar to the one at St. Vincent's. We did not know what lay behind the Garstang Road frontage, but we knew that this was a very large and important institution. In fact, behind the road frontage lay a sort of village set-up, with lovely Victorian villas set out like a village around a village green. The orphanage was opened in 1888 and could accommodate around 120 orphans, both boys and girls. Enlightened thinking at the time had decided that smaller units or homes would be far kinder to the orphans than impersonal, prison-like structures. We knew that the Harris family had been very important philanthropists for Preston and that down in town there was also a Harris Library and a Harris Institute.

Picture by Fr. Monk

Preston was a lively, cultured town. While Edmund was at Preston Catholic College, he was chosen to play the part of Lady Macbeth. He was a very good actor and looked marvellous in his medieval costume and stage make-up. We were very proud of him. Quite by chance, over fifty years later, while we were visiting a residential home for the elderly in Cumbria, one of the residents let it be known in conversation that she was 'Nutty' Almond, a former English teacher at Preston Catholic College and director of Edmund's Macbeth production. She also let it be known that her silk dressing gown had formed part of Edmund's stage costume. We also went to see a college production of *The Pirates of Penzance*, which was produced and performed to a highly professional standard. At Easter there was a Passion Play performed at night in the centre of the town. Huge crowds gathered to see the enactment and we went specifically to see Maurice, who had been chosen to take the part of one of the three kings.

One of the Jesuit teachers at the College was Fr Monk. Edmund taught us to refer to him by his college nickname of Addy. Addy was a very frequent visitor to our home. He had suffered from polio as a child and this had left him with one leg deformed and much shorter than the other. To compensate for this, he had custom-made black boots with a huge section of extra heel on one foot. We ourselves were able to benefit from the very vigorous programme of vaccination against polio and we all knew that one day we would have to line up for The Polio Prick and that this would be excruciatingly painful. Addy was a fanatically keen photographer and his favourite pastime was to come to our house on a Sunday afternoon and stay for tea, spending the afternoon chatting to us children. If it was a fine day, he would take the photographs in the garden. Addy was also a bit of a sketch artist. If there was a gap in the proceedings, he would whip out his sketch book. In just a few minutes he would produce a passable sketch of the garden, or a woodland or rural scene. Underneath the pencil-drawn picture he would write 'Happy Days'. I asked him how he had learned to draw and he explained that when he was ill with polio he was confined to bed alone for months. To make his confinement and solitude bearable he had taught himself to draw. As was usual in those days, he did all his photographic developing and printing himself and upon arrival at our house he would present us with the latest batch of photos.

In fact, if it was not for Addy, we probably would not have any photos of those Preston days. He perhaps saw himself as something of a society photographer, since there was nothing he liked better than to set us children up in staged pose. After tea, he would chivvy us children and organise us all to help with clearing the table, doing the washing up and drying and putting everything away. He loved to roll up his sleeves and do the washing up, chatting away the whole time. He taught us how to speed up the drying by taking two plates or saucers at a time on top of each other and then flipping them and drying them again. We were all brought up to help with setting and clearing the table, washing up and drying up and putting away. We were supposed to take it turns on a kind of rota. I had a reputation as being an expert dodger who could slip away just at the right time in order to evade my duties. When Fr Monk got back on his bicycle to cycle back to Winckley Square, we would all come out to the front to see him off. Addy would lower his bicycle to the side until it was almost horizontal, so that he could get on and then push off with his good leg. We boys found this hilarious and used to amuse ourselves with our bikes by seeing who could do the best impression of Fr Monk.

Dad used to talk a lot about a very respected colleague at Preston Catholic College called Joe Smith. It was always 'Joe Smith said this' and 'Joe Smith did such and such.' Joe Smith's passion was classical music. One Sunday afternoon Dad drove us all over to Joe Smith's house for tea. We were none too impressed by the scant and tasteless refreshments. We were even less impressed when we saw Joe Smith dragooning his large brood of highly talented children into an orchestral formation at one end of the dining room. They proceeded to inflict a series of classical pieces on us, the instruments including violin, cello, clarinet, and flute. This was intended as a treat, but was wasted on the Mohans, in whose lives classical music played no part whatsoever. Thereafter, the Concert at the Smiths was often recalled with horror. Joe Smith's son Ambrose went on to become a very successful Catholic school principal. By yet another strange quirk of fate, we were to get to know Ambrose's son Dominic through our nephew Joe Davenport, who had been a close friend of Dominic at school in Buxton and at college in Stockport.

Growing up in those 1950s years we did not feel that we were part of an olde-worlde, bygone age. On the contrary, we felt that we were up to the minute and part of an exciting new modern era. The P1 was a new jet fighter which was being built in Preston at English Electric. We boys enjoyed doing drawings of its distinctive sliced off circular nose, protruding cone, and sharp clipped straight-edged wings. We would love to spot it in the air above Fulwood as it completed its trials and test flights, leaving from Warton Aerodrome on the road to Lytham St Anne's. We knew that the P1 could break the sound barrier.

The country's very first motorway, a section of the M6 by-passing Preston, was opened in 1958 by Prime Minister Harold Macmillan. Coach trips were run from Preston so that people could experience the motorway. Some of Mum's friends came back and reported that it had been 'just like flying.'

In the late 1950s a major international trade fair took place in Preston. Mum and Dad referred to it as the Expo. Business representatives were to come from all over the world and translators were recruited to help European visitors to feel welcome. Mum applied for and got the job. We were all very proud of her, especially when she appeared in the local newspaper. It was a somewhat sexist photo-shoot, typical of the day, in which Mum and a bevy of attractive female fellow translators were made to sit in row with one knee over the other, wearing their tight-fitting short-cut corporate dresses, showing as much leg as possible and leaning forward with their arms by their sides. Mum really enjoyed the Expo experience. She earned a bit of pin money and it built up her confidence. She was about 35 years old at the time. Somehow, she must have managed to fit it in around all the demands of a 1950s housewife and mother of six.

In 1959 Dad moved on from Preston Catholic College and became the Deputy Head of Blessed Edmund Campion. This was a brand new Secondary Modern, a sign of the modernity and optimism of the post-1944 Education Act settlement, as well as a tribute to the self-confidence of the Catholic Church at that time and its commitment to an expanding role in secondary education. The school had just opened that year and was built on a green-field site between Cadley Causeway and Boys Lane, just a stone's throw from St Anthony's Church and the recently-built primary school.

Dad had more money now, plus his place of work was only a short distance from his home. Mum had always used a huge white cylindrical Hotpoint washing machine with built-in mangle on the top and a door below which you opened to remove the water.

She had large metal-hinged wooden washing tongs to fish out the clothes. There was a huge circular lid with a black handle which made a satisfying noise when you put it on and took it off. Now that the good times had arrived, it was out with the Hotpoint and in with the Hoover Twin Tub. The wooden tongs were now used to transfer the washed and rinsed clothes into the built-in spin dryer on the right-hand side of the rectangular structure. A rubber pipe was placed over the kitchen sink, a dial was then turned to 'drain', and we would watch with excitement as the machine magically leapt into life.

When you got to the Corner on the left-hand side of the road was a stop sign. It consisted of a white rectangle with HALT on it, with a red triangle above. Below were the letters F.U.D.C, which we knew stood for Fulwood Urban District Council. This told us that we lived in a real place, with its own affairs and its own local government. On the left-hand side of the Corner was the Co-Op. It was not yet a supermarket. Shopping there involved trudging from counter to counter. One day Mum asked Edmund what a supermarket was, and Edmund, who knew everything, explained it to Mum and how you would just go round and help yourself to everything off the shelves, then pay for it at the end. Mum did not like the sound of this at all. Each week 'The Order' would arrive from the Co-Op. This was a large rectangular cardboard box containing the week's food and groceries. It was delivered to the house by a nice friendly man in a smart brown overall. Drinks would arrive separately, delivered by the Drinks Lorry. This would be a strong wooden bottle crate and would contain glass bottles of Dandelion and Burdock, Lemonade and occasionally Tizer. The glass bottles would be saved and returned each week. As an alternative drink to the expensive bottled drinks, we would make up a fizzy drink from Creamola Foam. This was in a custard powder style tin and consisted of coloured crystals which you dissolved in water to make a fizzy drink, usually raspberry flavoured.

I was five years old when our German grandmother Omi came over to Preston to stay with us. She was there to help mum out during the confinement and the birth of her sixth child, which was to take place at home. When Mum went into labour upstairs in the front bedroom, we five children gathered around the shiny black table in the morning room and played board games. It was around six o'clock in the evening when Omi's face appeared round the door, with her hands touching her cheeks and tears in her eyes. '*Ein Mädchen, Kinder! Gott sei Dank, ein Kleines Mädchen!*' Madeleine Elizabeth was born on the 25th September, 1957.

Omi, with Maurice, Veronica, and Edmund

Chapter 9

Growler

And Uncle Giggi

I f any of us think or talk about Dad, it will not take us long to get onto the subject of his cars. This topic is closely connected to the issue of money, of which Dad, even as he began to earn more, never seemed to have enough. His first car was an Austin, red below and white above, registration VN 7295. Dad was so excited when he bought this car that he took us all out straightaway for a spin. Our destination was the Forest of Bowland, a beautiful area approached via the Ribble Valley and somewhat akin to the Lake District. I don't know whether Dad really was driving fast, but in our eyes, he was speeding like a maniac along the narrow country lanes. It was a matter of pride to Dad that, as an ex-serviceman, he had been exempt from taking the Driving Test. Five of us were crammed on the tiny bench-style back seat, obviously with no seat belts. We travelled standing up most of the time, clinging to each other and to whatever we could, including the string netting attached to the roof lining. Dad ignored our screams and yells and went faster and faster over the 'lily-bumps', the term used when the car nearly left the tarmac as it flew over a hump in the road, turning our stomachs over and making us want to go to the toilet.

VN7295   -   The Austin 16 Chalfont Limousine was manufactured from 1927 to 1937

We did on one occasion have a serious accident. Dad was driving along a deserted single-track road with drainage ditches on either side of the road. Some young bloods in a far superior vehicle came speeding towards us in the opposite direction. Dad was forced to take evasive action and the Baby Austin ended up on its side in the ditch, with all of us thrown on top of each other and screaming. The other car sped off, its occupants laughing and jeering out of the windows. Dad did not seem too worried and we all managed to climb our way out of the doors of the car. I don't know how we got home but we had a long walk before we could get help. Dad had to give a statement to the police, which started with the words 'I was on my way to Delaney's to get a new car' and was later read out solemnly in court. Dad always loved to quote these words.

Second in the succession of Dad's cars, but in first place in terms of its importance in our lives and affections, was CWE 842. This enormous Austin Six, which went by the name of Growler, had reputedly been retired after many years' service as a London taxi.

Rear view of Growler with GB sign

Huge rounded mudguards at the front, slightly dented. Enormous round headlights, which Dad would later paint yellow before we set off for 'The Continent'. Running boards. A hinged luggage rack at the back, which folded down and out to hold trunks and suitcases. In the rear compartment Growler had two seats which were built in three sections and which folded out from Mum and Dad's front seats. The seat behind Dad was for Veronica and the seat behind Mum was for Edmund. From his seat Edmund would keep a constant eye on the dashboard and on Dad's driving, especially on long journeys. Just like his father, Edmund would have a life-long love of large cars, and a passion for driving, especially in France. From her seat, again on long journeys abroad, Veronica would take it upon herself to administer shoulder massages to Dad to relieve his tension. Growler's seats were leather and smelled wonderful. Not so wonderful was the petrol leak in the rear cabin, where we gradually turned sick from breathing in noxious petrol fumes.

In order to keep Growler's tank-grade bodywork in tip-top condition Dad somewhat irrationally and randomly invested in the Nenette Dust Absorbing Polisher. This was a brush, about 10 inches in length, and similar to a floor mop, with a fine polished wooden handle. The Nenette was impregnated with a car polishing oil. When not in use, it lived in a metal container with a picture of a shiny car on it, with sun-like rays radiating out behind it. I cannot recall Dad ever touching the Nenette, but we boys loved it and regarded it as our possession. We would regularly get it out of the garage and polish the car, especially the vast bonnet and mudguards.

One of my prized Dinky Toys, when we lived in Preston, was a model of a 3-ton Beford army truck with detachable hood over the rear section. Dad had driven one of these during the war, which meant I could play with it pretending to snake my way through the sunken lanes of Normandy. One day I left this truck out on the drive after I'd been playing with it. Dad came home in Growler and ran over it, squashing it completely flat. I could not believe that he could be so cruel and callous as to smash my beloved Bedford truck. It was entirely my fault and typical of me to be so careless and forgetful as to leave something like that in the middle of the drive.

Growler with family, location unknown.

Edmund, Francis peeping, Maurice, Bernadette, Veronica, Madeleine in the arms of person unknown, possibly Uncle Hans Ollesch, husband of Omi's sister Tante Lischen

Growler spent a lot of his time not working. An essential piece of equipment for every car owner of that time was the Crank Handle, which would be slotted into a shaft by means of a hole through the grille. Dad would spend hours wrestling with the crank handle and turning over the engine, often to no avail. It was once decided that we would have a wonderful Sunday day out with the Moxhams, another large Catholic family who did not live far away but had a more prosperous life than we did. Mr Moxham was a large, handsome man with dark, lacquered hair, fine moustache, and muscular bearing. There were lots of Moxham children, including two very good-looking twins called Joseph and Mary. The jewel in the Moxham crown, with her lustrous dark hair and perfect pale skin, was their eldest daughter Helen. Came the day, the inevitable happened. Growler would not start.

Mr Moxham, like Dad, was ex-military and well used to setbacks of this kind. They spent most of the morning tinkering until Growler finally leapt back into life. Spark plugs, of which Growler had six, were usually at the root of the problem. When we eventually set off, we children were mixed up in the two cars. Mr Moxham's vehicle was as handsome as he was, the weighty chrome-laden Humber Super Snipe. I had the thrill not just of being in the same car as Helen, but of actually sitting next to her. We stopped to fill up with petrol and Helen, in polished tones, said 'Oh, please, could someone open the window. I absolutely adore the smell of petrol!' I could only gasp at the poise and sophistication of such a creature.

Dad's cars and Dad's camping were inextricably linked, the two defining pillars of his personality and the central formative experiences of our family years. Growler's first real trip was the famous camping holiday to Scotland, for which Dad set out without any actual tents. It was true that he had been lent a tent by the Porters, a family who lived in Regent's Drive. The Porter Tent turned out to be tiny and covered in sticky black tar waterproofing, so it was quickly discarded. Our King's Drive friends, the Kerrs, had told us that their uncle in Kirkcudbright had a double-decker bus we could all stay in. When we got to his farm the bus was there alright, but in a state of dereliction. It had faded blue bodywork and green moss and mildew on the windows. Dad drove us all off into town, parked Growler randomly in the town centre and wandered off, leaving us in the car not knowing what was going on. This happened all the time. We were quite used to spending long periods of time just sitting in Growler not knowing where Dad had gone or what he was up to. Mum and Dad's very occasional ventures out to country pubs to the north of Preston usually ended with the same scenario. Mum and Dad disappeared into the pub, leaving us fighting and arguing with each other in the locked car. If we were very lucky, Dad would emerge from the pub after about half an hour and rap on the car window. We would wind the window down; a clutch of crisp packets was hurled into the vehicle and we were left to fight over them.

On this occasion, Dad turned up having bought two magnificent tents, which he dumped on top of us. The *Windover* had a large central space and an inner tent on either side, one for the boys and one for the girls. The *Bukta Plover* was a beautiful, capacious ridge tent just for Mum and Dad. Our first use of the tents was on the banks of Loch Lomond, a very successful camping experience. One night Dad decided to drive into the nearest town to get fish and chips. It was late in the evening and getting dark. We three boys went out to the road and sat in a row on a wall, waiting for Dad to come back with the fish and chips. As the headlights of the passing cars came into view, we would state whether we thought they were Dad's. It was hard to mistake the huge circles of Growler's headlamps.

On the front step of 62 King's Drive

Edmund, Madeleine, Uncle Günther, Veronica in Bavarian costume, Francis, Bernadette, Maurice

62 King's Drive had a long drive to the right of the house, reaching from the front gate to the garage, in front of which Dad parked Growler. He used to drive Growler straight in and reverse out. Once, when he did this, he forgot to notice that opposite our drive, on the other side of the road, was parked a neighbour's pride and joy, a brand-new blue and white Triumph Herald. Dad reversed slowly and purposefully, moving inexorably in the direction of the Herald, Growler's rear luggage rack delivering a hefty broadside to the Herald, which crumpled like a biscuit tin. Dad went mad, not with himself but with us, and with some justification. Three or four of us had been kneeling on the back seat and watching out of the rear window, letting the whole incident play out before our eyes in slow motion and loving every second of it. Growler emerged completely unscathed from the encounter. Or if Growler had acquired a dent or two, that certainly was not going to worry Dad, who was very proud of his truck-bashing army days.

Our second holiday to Scotland was a much more ambitious affair than our earlier foray to Kirkcudbright. This time we had an extra passenger, Uncle Günther, or Giggi, as we used to call him then. This beloved uncle was still in the process of recovering from his wartime imprisonment with the Russians. He was rather thin and pale and tremendous fun. He loved us children and we would not leave him alone. He and Dad were very fond of each other and perhaps Günther was the nearest thing Dad ever had to a brother. Günther was a keen photographer and an early exponent of the new photographic phenomenon of slides. For the rest of his life, he would like nothing more than putting on a slide show of his "holiday in Schottland with Growler and Frank." Where he sat in the car I have no idea, nor where he slept in the tents. Almost all the camping on this holiday was wild camping. For toilet facilities each of us was issued with a garden trowel and sent off into the woods or wilderness to do our business.

A terrifying incident took place in Scotland. Baby Madeleine toddled off on her own and stood right on the edge of a deep concrete harbour, with a precipitous drop down to filthy water about forty feet below. We had to tiptoe up to her without startling her and quickly gather her up to safety.

The *Windover* had four poles all in a straight line. In order to put it up, Veronica, Maurice, me, and Bernadette would have to stand and hold the poles upright, with the entire outer tent hanging over us, while Dad, with Edmund's help, secured the pegs all around the bottom outside edge.

In fact, I think Dad did the guy ropes first, looping them over the metal protruding from the top end of the pole. Dad never gave you any warning. Suddenly you would be yanked violently to one side as he tugged on the guy rope and hammered the peg in. It was suffocating inside the canvas. The tent pegs were made of wood, and Dad, who liked to go over the top with everything he did, would regularly curse the tent pegs, as they shivered into pieces under the weight of his heavy army veteran blows with the wooden mallet.

Yes, it is very hard to separate the topic of Dad's cars, his camping, and his character. His character was cavalier and this was his approach to cars and to camping. And this was what our childhood was made of, Dad's camping holidays in a succession of Dad's cars.

1959 - Camping in Scotland with Growler and the Bukta Plover

The girls: Veronica (10), Madeleine (almost 2), Bernadette (almost 6)

The boys: Maurice (9), Edmund (12), Francis (7)

Chapter 10

St Pius X School

And the Woodland Walk

B y 1959 Maurice and I had been rescued from the limitations of St Vincent's and transferred to St Pius X, a private school aimed at giving boys the best possible preparation for entry either into Preston Catholic College or into Stonyhurst boarding school, also run by the Jesuits. Of all the gifts that my father gave to me and to my brother Maurice, and of all the things he did for us, this was one of the greatest, that he sent us to St Pius X Preparatory School. We had a very smart uniform, grey jacket with yellow and white piping around the lapels, down the front, across the top of the pockets and in a circle around the crest on the blazer pocket. The crest consisted of the Chi-Rho in white embroidery, representing the first letters of the name of Christ in Greek, and the name of Pius X in Latin, as well as the Latin word for Peace. There was even yellow piping around the cuffs of the sleeve of the blazer. There was also a matching grey jumper, grey shorts, matching grey socks with yellow and white stripes and a grey tie with green and gold stripes.

St Pius X had been founded in 1955 by a group of Preston businessmen, some of whose sons were pupils at the school. One of them, who was in my class, whose name I think was Arrowsmith, told me that his father virtually owned the school and therefore could bomb the school out of existence if he so chose. I was never quite sure why his father would ever wish to do this. Dad had a very close friendship with the school's headteacher, Gerard Georgeson. The fees were £21 a term, which would be the equivalent of £510 today. I think this might have been a reduced rate. Originally the school had started in a large red-brick Victorian house almost in the grounds of St Vincent's and possibly part of the original site. In 1962 St Vincent's was demolished and Maurice and I would stay behind after school for hours, standing by a fence and watching bulldozers and tractors pulling down our former school. Mr Georgeson came out and stood with us and said 'Of course, these vehicles are machines of solid steel.'

Wearing the St Pius X tie and jumper

We passed this comment on to Dad who found it very amusing and liked to repeat it whenever he could. This experience left us with a long-standing tendency to carry out demolition re-enactments with our cars and trucks. We would build structures out of wooden bricks and then hook a string from one of our toy tow trucks and carefully select points from which to tug, making all the appropriate vehicle engine noises. Maurice and I shared the excitement of moving with the school into Oak House, a beautiful old Victorian mansion set in its own grounds on the East side of the Garstang Road, set back from, but facing, the road. The school still occupies the site today and still nurtures the same civilised and compassionate ethos created seventy years ago by a remarkable educator who was years ahead of his time.

I made a friend at St Pius X called Joseph Osbaldeston. Joseph had a mass of freckles on his face and a mop of wild red hair above, with the broadest of grins, enormous ears, and bright blue eyes. Joseph and his family were obsessed with all things American. On Monday mornings Joseph would tell me proudly that he had spent the whole weekend listening to Elvis. I had little idea who Elvis was. I never sought Joseph out as a friend and we had absolutely nothing in common. He was an only child and I think he adopted me as a sort of hopeless ingenue who needed to be brought up to speed on modern life. One day he told me that I needed to learn the art of self-defence and that he could teach me the quickest and easiest way to disarm an opponent. It took just two simple steps. Step 1 was to punch them in the stomach. This would cause the opponent to double forward in pain, which was the opening to administer step 2, a karate chop on the back of the neck. He advised me to repeat steps one and two until I was satisfied that the opponent was disabled.

Hence the unprovoked attack on Simon Butler, whom I had chosen to be the guinea pig on whom I would practise. I waited behind the brick gate post of No 62 for Simon to come past on his way back from the Corner. On Monday morning I was able to report back to my mentor that his tuition had been very effective. To my utter amazement, three sets of stomach punches and karate chops, delivered in rapid succession on an unsuspecting and innocent by-passer had reduced my victim to a blubbering wreck and sent him scuttling off home. Unknown to me, Mum had been observing the whole incident. 'Francis, I have seen you doing the most terrible things.' But it did not go much further than that and I did not get reprimanded or punished either by my own parents or by those of the hapless victim. The next Saturday I had a genuine sin to take to Confession.

Joseph Osbaldeston had a further obsession, besides Elvis, which was the Assault Course. I have no idea where it was or how we were allowed to gain unimpeded access to it, but we were able to walk to it, a distance of two or three miles. For months Joseph had evangelised relentlessly about the wonders of the Army Assault Course. He had spent many an art lesson drawing detailed plans with diagrams and sketches, which he would speedily hide under the official art assignment if Mr Greenwood, our teacher at the time, ever came on patrol up the classroom aisle. I certainly did not tell my parents where I was going on the Saturday we eventually agreed upon to meet up for my initiation into the Assault Course. It was perhaps left over from the war training days. It was incredibly impressive, a full-scale course with all the usual equipment and obstacles, including log rolls, cargo nets, brick walls and so on. The pièce de resistance was the rope jump, where one had to take hold of a knotted rope, swing over a deep moat of muddy water and leap off over the other side. Timing was everything. Inevitably and predictably, I failed to get my timing right. I released the rope early and went straight into four feet of freezing slimy water. Osbaldeston screamed at me for being such a fool, whilst also roaring with laughter. I had to walk several miles home in drenched and spattered clothes and explain to my mother how it had happened. Again, I have no recollection of being told off or reprimanded in any way. Thereafter Osbaldeston abandoned his project to turn me into a fellow commando and the Assault Course was never mentioned again.

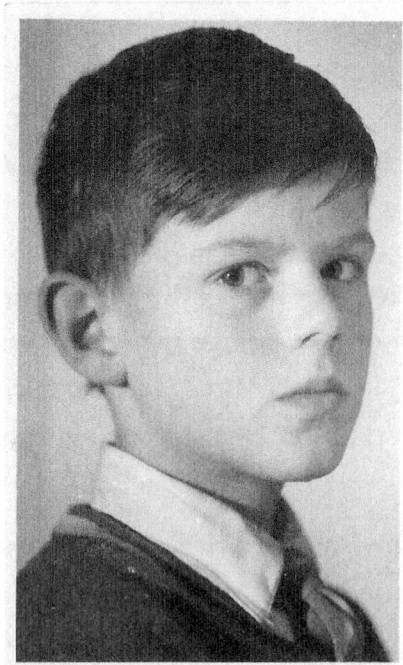

Mr Georgeson had read Classics at Bangor University and was quite passionate about etymology, always asking us whether we thought a particular word came from Greek or Latin. In fact, he was passionate about everything. His eyes burned with a benign but ferocious intensity and power. Like Dad, he had fought in the war. He sported a military moustache and spoke in the distinctive clipped tones of an army officer. He was interested in everything and wanted us to be as committed and curious about life as he was. In one corner of the beautiful oak-panelled hallway he would put up a print of a piece of art work by a famous artist such as Vermeer, Bosch, Rembrandt, Botticelli, Cézanne, Matisse, Van Gogh, Picasso. He was especially fond of Goya. He would gather us around the painting in small groups of ten or twelve. Without telling us anything about the painting he would ask for our opinions and let us talk freely and openly. He might finish up with a few comments and pointers about the date and context of the painting and things we might like to look out for and think about.

A vital part of our schooling was our reading diary. Mr Georgeson had built up an excellent library of books which were housed not in a library but on low shelves in the classroom alongside our desks. Significant time was set aside for us to read in silence, or to write up our reading log. These were not plot summaries but personal impressions and reflections on what the book had meant to us and what we felt we had learned. Mr Georgeson set great store by writing and worked on the assumption that every single one of us had the potential to be a writer. Our project in Junior 4 was to write a book. It was to be completed in our own time, in whatever form and on any topic or theme. He knew that the result would be immature and unsatisfactory. He also seemed to know that the attempt, and even the thought of the attempt, the very intention to write and the belief that it might be possible, would give a boost to our self-esteem and personal development.

At some point a light must be switched on in a young person's mind and a flame of learning must be lit. Mr Georgeson knew that an education would not be worth the name without this. In fact, when he went round the class and asked us what topic we had chosen I proudly said 'Cowboys.' He was not dismissive of this and he knew that I had been reading a magnificent non-fiction book on Cowboys from the class library. He waited until he could speak to me quietly afterwards on a one-to-one basis and gently suggested to me that it might be better 'to write about what you know.' I readjusted my plans and decided to write about my daily walk to school. This involved little descriptions of the dog poo on the pavement, of the trees along the grass verges, of the magnificent frontage of the Kerr residence, of a gloomy house which we decided was haunted and which we used to run past at top speed, of the long fence on the other side of the road as you came to the Garstang Road, behind which a dog barked ferociously and followed you all along the length of the boundary. I described how I would pretend the pavement was an American freeway and I was in a huge sedan, or on another day King's Drive became a lonely mountain track and I was in a battered ex-army Land Rover. Sometimes I was in a Sherman tank, the pieces of dog poo were landmines to be avoided. Mr Georgeson was much happier with this and said 'You know, I think you're really on to something here.'

He was a great believer in art and craft as well as on technology. We might be given a whole afternoon to develop a painting. One or two pieces of work were then displayed on the classroom wall. I did a painting of Guy Fawkes in the cellars beneath the Houses of Parliament. It was a close-up of his head, with beard and Jacobean hat. He was holding a flickering candle to light his way through the tunnels and this cast a shadow on the grey stone wall behind. An iron ring was fixed to the wall behind. This was greatly admired and found its way to the classroom wall. Mr Georgeson also taught us to weave. We got a piece of strong card, around A5 in size, and made a neat jagged edge at the top and the bottom end. The warp was then put in place around both sides of the card, using the jagged points on each end of the card to hold the wool in place. We then made a shuttle out of another piece of card and used this to pass the weft through. Two more pieces of card were used in turn to raise the strings of the warp so that the weft could be passed through. In the end you had a rectangle of woven wool which could then be used as a mat for a teapot. We could use whatever colours we wanted, begging the wool of our mothers. Mine consisted of horizontal stripes in white and salmon pink.

Mr Georgeson also taught us to sew. We learned how to thread a needle, sew on a button, and do two types of stitch, a simple running stitch, which was actually very difficult to get neat and straight, and a hemming stitch. Alongside this we learned how to use papier mâché as a cheap way to make very strong and stable structures. Our project was to make a glove puppet. We each brought in a light bulb and this was to make the puppet's head. Plasticine was added to create nose, ears, and chin. The bulb was then smeared with Vaseline and covered in several layers of gloopy papier mâché. While that was drying for a couple of days, we concentrated on sewing the glove puppet, using our hands to measure the material, and cutting out two identical templates, to be sewn together. A craft knife was used to cut open the papier mâché head and remove the light bulb. The two halves of the head were then reunited and fixed with more papier mâché. The glove puppet material was fixed to the head with a rubber band which was sewn on and hidden. We could then add buttons to the front of the glove puppet and maybe a collar and cuffs. For my character I chose a Mr Pastry type character, using cotton wool to create the tufts of white hair around the bald head. We then had to write little scripts and perform to each other in small groups and then to the class.

One day Mr Georgeson gave us a lesson about suspension bridges and explained to us that a magnificent suspension bridge was to be built across the Severn Estuary. He also taught us about all the different types of bridges, such as the arched bridges of the Tyne and Sydney Harbour. I went home and cut up a Corn Flakes packet to create the basic structure. I took needle and thread from Mum's Benson and Hedges sewing tin and used this to make suspension cables. I managed to get the finished product into school the next day, but it got rather badly damaged when I put it in my desk and shut the lid. I stayed behind at the end of the day and got it out to see if I could repair it. Mr Georgeson came back into the classroom and saw that I was crying. He understood the situation immediately and was full of enthusiasm about what I had made. He got me to explain in my own words how I had gone about making it. He then took it in his hands and manipulated it, demonstrating to me that it was functioning exactly how a suspension bridge was supposed to function, with each force or tension countered and balanced by an opposing and equal force. I had made the bridge, but it was not until Mr Georgeson demonstrated it that I really understood its significance.

He loved music and one day he asked the class if their parents had any classical records at home. These were very early days for someone to have a gramophone collection. One boy put up his hand and said 'My Mum and Dad have got the one that goes Boom! Boom!' 'Oh, marvellous,' said Mr Georgeson, 'That'll be the 1812 Overture by Tchaikovsky.' The record was duly supplied and used for the first of many classical music sessions. Mr Georgeson had a headteacher's flat at the school and the whole class gathered in his living room and sat on the carpet and listened to the stirring music. This was my first classical music experience and from then on, I would be a huge fan of Tchaikovsky.

We did PE and Sport at St Pius X but it always seemed to be something to enjoy and not to dread, an opportunity for relaxation, not humiliation. Mr Georgeson was a former soldier and a very masculine character, but he understood very well that boys are complex creatures, each with a spectrum of masculine and feminine gifts and needs. He wanted us to enjoy the natural world and to find solace and refreshment in the open-air environment. For this reason, he created the Woodland Walk. This was a beautiful walk through a stretch of woodland which lay on the southern edge of the Oak House estate. Two prefects guarded the entrance to the path at the Garstang Road side so that the boys entering the Woodland Walk were monitored. We were not allowed to go through the walk alone, but had to go in pairs and never in a group. This gave us a chance to get some gentle exercise and was greatly appreciated as an alternative to playing football. It was an opportunity to have a decent conversation. It helped us to grow up, to make choices and to be responsible.

Five minutes before the start of afternoon school a prefect would stand at the entrance to the toilets and ring a hand bell. This was the Dirty Paws Bell, the signal for every single boy to go to the toilet and wash their hands thoroughly, ready for the start of afternoon school. Sometimes at lunchtime, especially when we were in the younger years, we would bring Dinky Toys in to play with on the ground or walls. We were not really permitted to bring toys into school but we would find a quiet corner and play happily. Maurice and I would save up our pocket money, and any money that was given to us, and buy our own Dinky Toys from Mrs Corbett. She had a smart cardboard display unit in her shop window, with the word Dinky Toys in red on a yellow banner background, which showed off an ever-changing collection of desirable models.

We could also ask her for the Dinky Catalogue, which gave a more comprehensive list of all the current models available. Things took a giant leap forward in 1959 when Independent Suspension was introduced. This technical innovation was swiftly followed in 1960 with Fingertip Steering. My prized possession was a white 3.4 Jaguar Police Car, whose special features were listed on the box as Windows, Fingertip steering, Seats, Steering wheel, 4-Wheel Suspension, Police Crew, Radio Aerial, and Flasher Beacon. I brought this into St Pius X to show it off to my friends. Maurice and I were Dinky Toy buddies and would spend many happy hours either inside or outside playing with our cars. Maurice was highly adept at creating edgy semi-urban settings, consisting of alleyways, warehouses, scrap yards and wood yards, with cars abandoned in shadowy corners. I preferred open road and country scenery type settings and would borrow mum's clothes pegs to create highways and road junctions. The great rival to the Dinky Toy was the Corgi collection. Corgi models were a cut above Dinky Toys, being made of a heavier grade metal and having a superior finish. However, we were generally very loyal to Dinky, as being more economical and somehow more friendly and with a greater variety and range. Dinky Toys were made by Meccano Ltd in Liverpool, while Corgi were made by Mettoy in Northampton.

Mr Georgeson decided that I had acting skills and asked me to do an assembly. Oak House had a beautiful square hall right in the centre of the building and we used this both for dining and for assemblies. He gave me a copy of *Old Possum's Book of Practical Cats* and asked me to stay after school for just 15 minutes so that he could hear a read-through and give me some tips for improvements. I did not tell my parents or anyone at home that I was doing this. When I came to perform it, I think it went quite well, but I got the distinct impression that while it delighted Mr Georgeson it was quite inaccessible to the rest of the school. The main thing I remember is my stagey shaking of my hand for the line '*And he suffers from palsy which makes his paws shake.*'

Our schooling was based on the competitive principle. Our end of term reports listed our position in the class. We were given exams every single term so that we were used to them. The same pale blue report book was sent home with a new page filled in for all the subjects. My rival in my class was Ralph Seed, who always went home as First in Class.

I had no real desire to beat him. It was obvious to me that he was far more intelligent than I was. He was also my friend with whom I got on very well. He was a delightful young man with black hair and freckles and an extremely quiet, calm, and dignified manner. Just once I gained the position of First in Class. Neither Ralph nor I were particularly bothered or interested and neither Mr Georgeson nor my parents made any fuss about it. However, I did receive a prize in the form of a book. It was called *Seabird* and had been written just after the war. It was a seafaring story dealing with the whaling industry and set in the Hawaiian Islands. The 1960 edition I received was illustrated with stunning drawings and artwork. I loved this book and read it again and again, finding it very mysterious, getting lost in the pictures and never quite understanding it. The seabird was made of wood, carved on board a whaler in 1832 by a man called Ezra. It was then passed on through four generations, right through to 1948. Beneath my prize certificate was the inscription:

Many good ships have sailed the seas
since Ezra carved the SEABIRD.
Hoisted on a Sperm Whale's jaw,
ye'll find the log of her voyagings.

I still treasure this book today. Leaving Preston meant leaving my friend Ralph Seed. I met up with him again at Cambridge many years later. He was exactly the same as he had been at St Pius X eight years earlier, when he had already effectively been a young adult.

One of the major aims of the prep school was to prepare us for our 11 plus, so that we could gain entry to the grammar school of our choice, which in our case meant either Preston Catholic College or Stonyhurst. We did a lot of drilling in 'the three Rs', especially in the mornings, but our success and progress in preparation for the 11 plus was placed in our own hands. We had a carefully graded succession of work books, with pale, patterned covers in pastel pink and green and yellow. These took us through a thorough programme of preparation in arithmetic, numerical and spatial reasoning, vocabulary, grammar, spelling, comprehension, verbal reasoning and writing skills. Maurice and I both absolutely loved these books and encouraged each other as we cheerfully worked our way through them, which was no effort at all.

The workbooks were written with a complete comprehension of the requirements of the 11 plus examination and it would be unimaginable to attempt the 11 plus without this systematic familiarisation with all its styles of questioning. Mr Georgeson would keep track of our work books as we completed them and would issue us with the new ones. It was mainly for this service that parents were paying for a private prep school education.

Edmund was always on hand to help me with my school work if required. He would do this in a very calm and efficient manner. In those days we often used to ask a sibling to test us on our work. One day we were doing the Romans at school and had just done the chapter on Hadrian's Wall. We were going to have a test the following day so I asked Edmund to test me. 'How long is the Wall?' was his first question. 'Foot by foot, yard by yard, mile by mile, the Wall grew, until it stretched from the Solway Firth all the way to the mouth of the River Tyne.' was my answer. Edmund roared with laughter and explained to me how important it was when studying just to go for the essential facts and not waste time with anything else. Writing an 'Essay', which was an exercise in creative writing, was an important part of our schooling in those days. Mum used to say that Edmund's essays were the shortest in the class.

A favourite afternoon activity was the Spelling Bee. The class would be divided into two and each side would elect a team of three. Members of the 'audience' of each side could then take it in turns to pose a spelling to the opposing team. We would often start with 'encyclopaedia' or 'parallelogram' or 'antidisestablishmentarianism'. Mr Georgeson would stand back and allow the boys to run the whole show, with tellers keeping score on the blackboard and a pupil official running the dictionary and adjudicating the responses.

One of the things that brought Gerard and Lynne Georgeson together with Mum and Dad was their shared love of camping. The Georgesons were pioneers of European motoring and camping, long before such things were spoken of or even thought about. The Georgesons would come round to our house and share tips on where to buy camping equipment and what items were best to bring with you abroad. They would share funny stories of their camping mishaps and adventures, of which there were always many. Being a Europhile, Gerard bought a VW Beetle and was very proud of owning a complete set of metric as opposed to Imperial spanners. Like all ex-servicemen, and perhaps all men of the 1950s, he expected to have to tinker with a car engine and attempt his own repairs.

In the early 60s the Georgesons had toured all the way through Communist Yugoslavia and had cracked open the sump of their vehicle on a rocky country road. Just like Dad, Gerard Georgeson was happiest sporting his army shorts and messing about in the open air. The Georgesons had three children, Hilary, Mark, and Philippa. They were older than us and somewhat frightening as they were so intelligent.

At school Mr Georgeson helped us boys to be aware of the outside world. He told us about the conflict between France and Algeria and explained to us about the OAS, *L'Organisation Armée Sécrète*, which was carrying out atrocities and attacks in Paris as part of its struggle for independence for Algeria. He told us how he had been to Mass in Paris and seen the letters OAS daubed on the front of the altar.

When I was in Junior 3 Mr Georgeson taught us in a very large classroom on the first floor with a fine bay window overlooking the right-hand side of the house toward the garden and woodland. Mr Georgeson created a large crib and mounted it on his desk at the front of the room in the centre. He then got some spare desks and put them all together in a long line leading from the crib to the bay window, It was just like a catwalk. He then asked each of us to bring in something from home which was precious to us and which had some character, like a cuddly soft toy or a teddy bear or anything we thought was appropriate, no matter what the size. All we had to do was bring it in and place it on the catwalk, which had been covered with crêpe paper to make a kind of path or roadway or red carpet. Each of our gifts or symbols was to be placed on the causeway, pointing towards the crib. The arrangement meant that the classroom was effectively split in two. When we looked up from our work, or while we were listening to Mr Georgeson, for the whole of Advent, we would look at the crib, but also at the host of strange and extraordinary creations trotting along towards the crib. I chose a very unusual possession to represent myself. It was a plastic turtle only one or two inches in height, with a funny face and a green and yellow shell. He was on a flat base so that one leg was down and the other up, with both arms and legs in the running position. Mr Georgeson never commented on anything that we brought in and nor did any of the pupils make comments about each other's toys or cuddlies, which we were allowed to place wherever we wanted on the road.

This was the faith which Mr Georgeson shared with his pupils and this was how he shared it, through symbols, symbolic gestures, which he never explained or expounded on, allowing those under his care complete freedom and dignity in making their own personal response to Catholic belief and practice.

During 1959 Mr Georgeson began to tell us about something called the Second Vatican Council. It was being prepared at the moment and in two years' time every Roman Catholic bishop in the world would make the journey to Rome for a most marvellous meeting. They would discuss all sorts of things and they would help our church to keep up with all the changes in the modern world. They would work together with all the good people in the world who were not Catholics but who wanted to create a better world for us all to live in. He told us all about the liveliness of the Church in South America and about the new cathedral that was being built in Brasilia, the brave new capital of Brazil in the heart of the Amazon forest. In our RE books, we drew a picture of the incredible Metropolitan Cathedral of Our Lady that was under construction at the time. At the top of the pointed columns that reached into the sky, we wrote the gifts of the Holy Spirit, wisdom, understanding, counsel, fortitude, knowledge, piety, fear of God.

Gerard died before his time, I think sometime during the 1970s, while undergoing heart surgery. As a result, both he and his wife were denied the joy of a happy retirement together. I wrote a letter of condolence to Lynne. In her letter back to me, she said 'Gerard thought that because he enjoyed his work so much, he was immune to the effect it was having on him.'

Chapter 11

Normandy

And the 23rd Hussars

Dad was keen to take us on walks, or was so desperate on Sundays to find something to occupy us that a walk was the easiest solution. If we walked to the Corner the road on the other side of Black Bull Lane, carrying on in the same direction as King's Drive, was Boys Lane. King's Drive in the 1950s was almost at the northern boundary of Preston and countryside lay all around. Boys Lane was still a country lane, with huge tall trees on either side as it plunged down steeply into a hollow and then up the other side. Dad once told me, as we strolled down Boys Lane, that G K Chesterton used to imagine the trees as people with personalities all of their own. GK was of enormous importance to Dad and to many Catholics of his generation. Dad often liked to quote the story of G K Chesterton's wife receiving a telegram from her husband saying 'Am at Victoria. Where am I supposed to be?'

The highlight of a walk with Dad would be to egg him on to share some of his stories from the war. This was especially true of the walks we did on our camping trips, where Dad would take us out for a walk in the evening and when he had more time to talk to us and indulge us. He was at once both reticent and talkative about the war, neither bottling it all up unhealthily, not allowing himself to get carried away.

The centrepiece of Dad's wartime stories and experience was the Normandy campaign, which took place from June to August 1944. I grew up believing that Dad had landed on D-Day and would happily share this fact with others. Throughout our lives, from our earliest days, the official war history of Dad's regiment was sitting on our bookshelf in its bumpy green soft-back cover, If I had consulted this as a youngster, I would have found out in a few minutes of reading that Dad's regiment did not in fact land until 14th June. I only got it all straight in my head in August 2006, when I went to Normandy with my sons James and Timothy to research and retrace Dad's Normandy campaign on the ground.

Dad's Normandy stories started with the landing on the beach. This was Juno Beach, or Courseulles-sur-Mer, although Dad never told us this. It was the most easterly of the five Normandy beaches, between Gold and Sword, and started at the river estuary adjacent to Caen. Juno Beach encompassed the four coastal villages of Graye-sur-Mer, Courseulles-sur-Mer, Bernières-sur-Mer, and St. Aubin-sur-Mer. It had been taken by the Canadians at very considerable cost on 6th June.

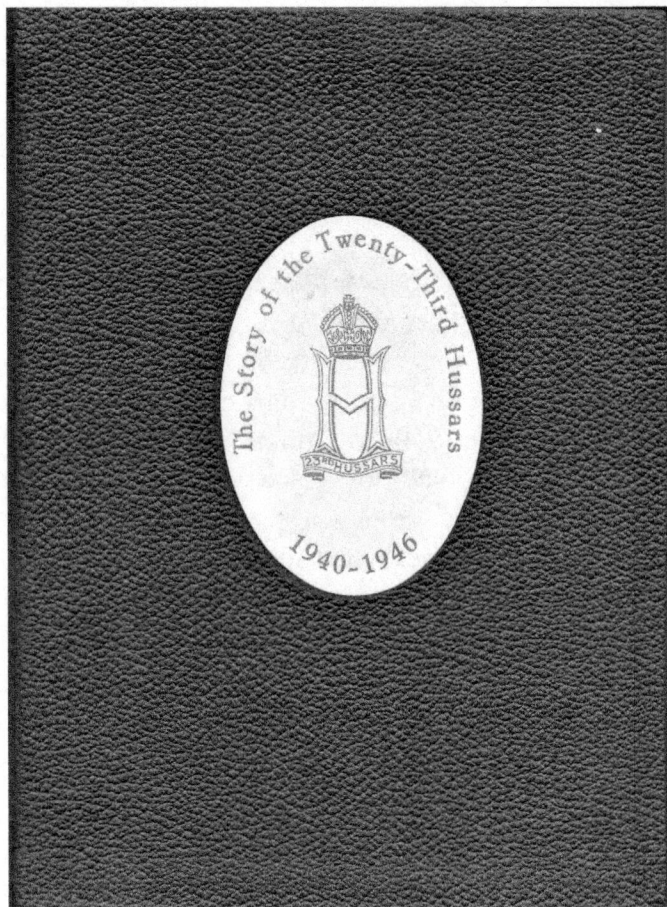

We knew from when we were tiny that Dad's unit was a tank regiment named the 23rd Hussars. It was only much later, when I read the book through, that I learned that the Hussars, together with the 3rd Royal Tanks, formed the 11th Armoured Division. We also knew that Dad's key role was as a member of the Royal Corps of Signals. He was very proud of the 23rd Hussars and his pride was completely warranted. They played an outstanding role in the battle for Normandy and in the subsequent drive through Belgium and Holland and into Northern Germany. Dad was even more proud of the Signals and it is probably fair to say that the technical and engineering side of the Signals appealed to him enormously, far more than the military combatant role. That does not mean that Dad was not in the fighting and not right in the thick of it, because he was. Like many British ex-servicemen, Dad did not dwell on the war, or glorify it in any way. His active service war was to last eleven months and in those eleven months Dad's brigade was involved in active contact with the enemy for all but five days.

Dad in battle dress, with Royal Signals badge and single stripe of Lance-Corporal. Unclear on the photo, but partly visible at the top of the arm, is the emblem of the 11th Armoured Division, the black bull on yellow background.

The Black Bull

23rd Hussars cap badge

In 1944 the regiment was based in Dad's home county of Yorkshire. On the regimental memorial in Bridlington can be read a long list of battle honours: Odon, Caen, Bas Perrier, Amiens, Antwerp, Helchteren, De Rips, Leunen, Usselstein, Givet, Bure, Ypres, Rhine, Legden, Stolzenau, Belsen, Luneburg, Lubeck.

Gosport was the harbour from which Dad embarked for war in France. The Hussars official history describes the regiment as consisting of 'civilians drawn haphazardly from all walks of life and from every corner of the British Isles.' Dad told us how he had trained in Scotland, how they had had to crawl across fields with live ammunition being fired over their heads, how eventually they had to gather secretly in the south of England and knew that this was it. It must be time for the invasion.

At the start of the war, early in the regiment's history, Dad was inspected by Winston Churchill. In 1944 the regiment received two further morale-boosting inspections, both of which took place in Bridlington. The first, in February, was from Montgomery, the second, in March, was from King George himself, accompanied by Princess Elizabeth and Princess Margaret. There is no doubt that Dad held Monty in high esteem and that Monty's was the inspection he was most proud of. The Hussars regimental history explains that Monty would give the same speech, following the same format all over the country. Having inspected the troops formally, he would then stand on a jeep and gather the troops around him informally, and would give the following speech:

'I wanted to come here today so that we could have a look at one another – so that I could have a look at you and you could have a look at me. We have a job to do together.'

The Hussars were down in Gosport by June 11th and boarded their LCTs on the night of 14th June.

On the following morning, in beautiful calm weather, they made their channel crossing Four days later, and for a whole week, a vicious storm was to break out in the channel, wrecking large parts of the Mulberry Harbour at Arromanches and making seaborne landings impossible. As Dad crossed the channel in a landing craft, a senior officer turned to him and said "For God's sake, Mohan, try and show a bit of interest. You do realise this is history we're making, don't you?" Dad rather prided himself on his nonchalance. Even before D-Day, he used to say to his comrades 'Of course, you know that the Germans are not our real enemy. The real enemy from now on is going to be the Russians.'

Juno Beach, pictured in 2006

Dad did not drive or fight in a tank. As a member of the Signals Corps, he drove and rode in a 5-ton truck. The story went that before leaving for France Dad and his fellow Signals men had worked hard to fit out their army truck and get it exactly as they wanted it. As they drove off the Landing Craft and onto the sands of Juno Beach, they heard incoming and decided to jump out of the truck and make a run for it. As they ran away over the sands they turned, to see their beloved home-from-home blown to kingdom come.

When Dad arrived in Normandy the allies had only managed to advance seven miles inland since D-Day. The big obstacle that lay in their path was the city of Caen, which the Germans were using as a defensive fortress. Dad loved this city very much and was always very happy to revisit it in later years. Montgomery came into the Normandy campaign with a superb reputation in tank warfare as a result of his victory over Rommel in North Africa. That was why the men had such confidence in him. However, Montgomery's progress in Normandy was painfully slow. According to the original battle plans, Caen was supposed to have been taken in the first one or two days of the campaign, but a direct attack on the city had to be abandoned. Before Dad arrived, Monty had tried to get around the city to the west, via Villers-Bocage, but that attack had ground to a halt.

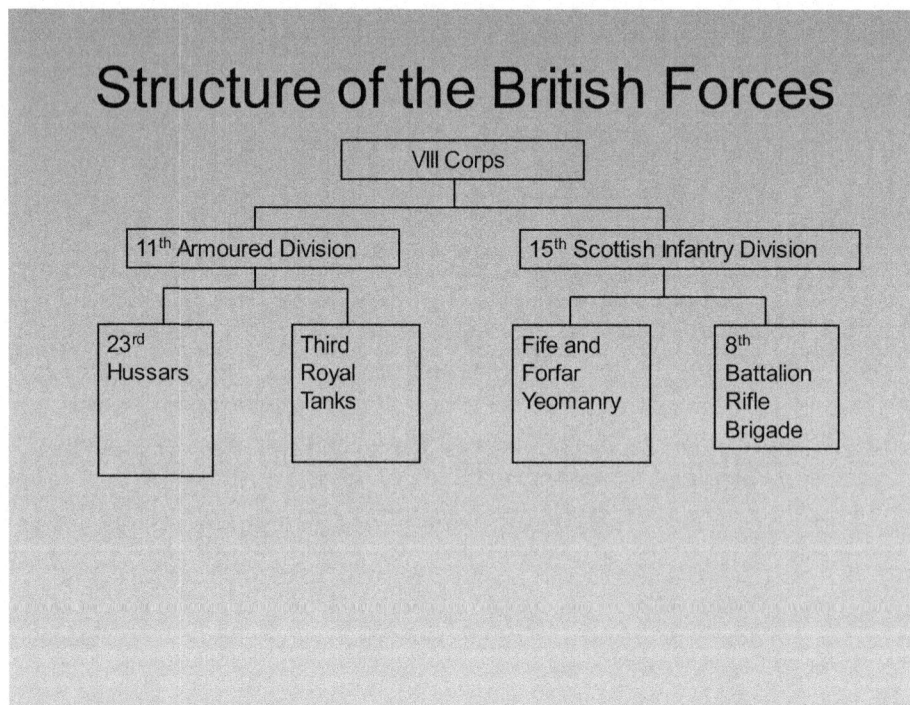

Structure of the British Forces

```
                        VIII Corps
            ┌───────────────┴───────────────┐
   11th Armoured Division          15th Scottish Infantry Division
      ┌─────┴─────┐                    ┌─────┴─────┐
   23rd        Third               Fife and      8th
   Hussars     Royal               Forfar        Battalion
               Tanks               Yeomanry       Rifle
                                                  Brigade
```

Dad's first military operation was Montgomery's third attempt to break out of the bridgehead and take Caen. It was codenamed Operation EPSOM and it ran from 26th to 29th June 1944. It involved 60,000 men, 600 tanks and 700 artillery. After crossing the Caen-Bayeux railway, the regiment halted for some time as the infantry ahead were advancing only slowly in the face of stubborn opposition. Dad's first day in battle saw some very bitter fighting. The tactics were crude, with infantry marching forward in First World War-style formation, while the tanks hung back behind.

One of Dad's proud reminiscences was that he had seen Scottish pipers playing their bagpipes as their troops advanced into battle. This memory is borne out by the fact that the Hussars worked closely with the Fife and Forfar Yeomanry, a Scottish infantry regiment.

One of Dad's reminiscences was that the very fiercest resistance that they ever met was when they encountered the Hitler Youth. I always imagined that this must have taken place in the final stages of the war, as they advanced into Germany. The fact is that the Hussars had come up against the Hitler Youth at the very first settlement they approached, the village of Cheux, on their very first day of active fighting. Dad said that even after they had been captured and disarmed, the Hitler Youth would continue to mock and harass the British Tommies, hurling abuse at them and swinging their arms to mock the way the British marched.

In the battle for Caen the Hussars were up against one of the most formidable of all German fighting units, the 12th SS Panzer, led by the notorious Colonel Kurt 'Panzer' Meyer. Kurt Meyer was a fanatical Nazi. After the war he received the death penalty for his atrocities against Canadian soldiers in Normandy. He was sentenced to be shot by a firing squad. Following an appeal, this sentence was commuted to life imprisonment.

James and Tim in Normandy

Point 112

In just two days, the 23rd Hussars and the 11th Armoured Brigade made significant territorial advances. They secured an important river crossing, the Odon, and in very bitter fighting, with the Hussars in the spearhead of the attack, they secured the strategic high ground of Point 112. Point 112 is still marked in Normandy today. The landscape around this high ground remains unchanged. The little hillside stands in eery isolation, with the German defensive ditches still gouged out of the earth at its crest.

The Hussars even withstood a massive counter attack of two SS Panzer Divisions which had just arrived from Russia. To capture Point 112 was a huge victory, achieved by ordinary citizen conscripts against battle-hardened professionals. For some unaccountable reason, General Dempsey, the overall British commander, and Montgomery's superior, decided to abandon Point 112 and withdraw back behind the Odon. The British lost everything they had gained in Operation EPSOM. In those three days of fighting, they had lost over 4000 men. Of these, 1,256 were from the 11th Armoured Division and of these 36 men from Dad's regiment died.

One of Dad's reminiscences was of a friend of his in the 23rd Hussars who spent all day every day saying that 'these generals haven't got a clue what they're doing." There was some justification for this point of view. Operation EPSOM, which cost so many lives, was already the third botched attempt to break out from the bridgehead and surround Caen. However, the actual performance of the 23rd Hussars in their first five days of action had been outstanding. It had been the Hussars themselves who had taken Point 112 from the Germans. When they arrived at the summit of Point 112, they had actually run out of ammunition, which shows the extreme nature of the fighting and the fact that it was a 'very close-run thing'.

Operation CHARNWOOD was a joint British and Canadian infantry operation, which represented a second attempt to batter a way into Caen, still defended by Kurt Meyer's 12th SS Panzer. The first part of the operation was very controversial, the virtual carpet bombing of the beautiful city of Caen. Not only was this controversial, it proved to be completely ineffective in making any impact on the German defences. It traumatised and alienated the French population. Thousands took refuge in the ancient cathedral, in whose nave lay the tomb of the Conqueror. A red cross was painted on the roof of the cathedral and people lived inside the church for days. Some commentators say that Montgomery's conduct of the whole European war was relatively inept, and in the opinion of some, a catalogue of disasters which destroyed his reputation. 3000 citizens of Caen died in allied air raids as part of Operation CHARNWOOD.

Normandy Bocage

For the first two weeks of July, the Hussars were able to rest and recuperate. They even found time to organize a sports day. On the 16th - 20th July, Monty made his fifth attempt to break the deadlock. It was called Operation GOODWOOD. When Dad took us on walks down country lanes, especially at dusk or at night, he would tell us how in Normandy they had had to make their advances and forward movements at night-time. They were not allowed to use any form of lights, so they would navigate by looking up out above the bocage to see the summer night sky. The regiment moved round the north side of Caen at night time on the 16th July and crossed the River Orne by means of a Bailey Bridge just near the famous Pegasus Bridge, captured just after midnight on D-Day by the Sixth Airborne Division. The concentration area for Operation GOODWOOD was among the wreckage of the gliders which had landed on the 6 June. When all the tanks and armoured vehicles had gathered in readiness for the battle, they filled one square mile. They looked impressive, but the size of the attacking force was the problem. They ended up in one huge traffic jam, presenting an easy target for the enemy. The Germans knew in advance the exact time and date of the attack. Operation GOODWOOD was a complete disaster. It was General Dempsey's idea, but Montgomery had bought into the idea, hoping for a dramatic breakthrough all the way through to the Falaise. The 11th Armoured Division lost 400 tanks, 36% of its total number. 106 of the 23rd Hussars' tanks were destroyed. 25 men were killed.

Up next was Operation BLUECOAT, which was to run from 30th July to 12th August. It was Dad's third major battle, and for Montgomery, his sixth attempt to break out from the bridgehead. He was under pressure from all sides, especially the Americans, who had been battling their way down from the Cherbourg peninsular and from the western beaches and were desperate to link up with the British and Canadian advance. It was in this operation that the 23rd Hussars were to find themselves in a nightmare situation, advancing 'a bridge too far', getting completely cut off from their supply lines, and spending several days and nights, surrounded by the enemy.

Operation BLUECOAT began at the town of Caumont and started well. At a village called La Ferrière, the Hussars received the sort of liberation welcome sometimes depicted on Second World War films, with jubilant villagers and pretty girls plying them with flowers and drinks of cider. The soldiers had been issued with strict instructions to treat French women with respect and caution. Dad explained that he and his fellow soldiers would get shaved every single morning without fail, usually in cold water, no matter what the conditions were or what the situation was that they found themselves in.

One day, as they were stopped in Normandy, Dad and his mates saw some chickens and decided to shoot one with a Sten gun. This proved far harder than they thought and after expending a few magazines of ammo they were forced to give up. Dad and his colleagues did not have all that much time for the Normandy farmers. When the soldiers went to a farm for help in the form of food or drink, the farmers would be most unhelpful and say that there was no food or drink there and that they themselves were starving. The British soldiers would then find huge stashes of food and drink and all sorts of supplies. The French would then shrug their shoulders and say that they had been hiding it all from the Boche.

Le Beny Bocage

It was a beautiful sunny afternoon, 1st August 1944, when the Hussars got into the stone-built hillside settlement of Le Beny Bocage. This is an idyllic village to visit today, arranged in iconic French fashion around a beautiful town square, complete with an ornate water fountain and covered market. Just around the corner, as you come down off the ridge from Le Beny Bocage, is a tiny military cemetery called Saint Charles de Percy. A sign at the cemetery states: These men died in Operation BLUECOAT in August 1944. Here among the hundreds of gravestones you can find the names of men Dad might well have known: B Richardson, age 32, A Withers, age 24, C Moore, age 22, J G Stock, age 21, F J Sibbring, age 20, A E Terry, age 20. Dad himself was aged 26.

The 'bridge too far' scenario is called the Battle of Le Bas Perrier. It remains exactly as it was in 1944, with the entire landscape unchanged.

Scene of the Battle of Le Bas Perrier

The battlefield is marked today with an impressive monument on which can be read the name of Major General GPB Roberts, known to his men as 'Pip' Roberts. Philip Roberts was only 37 years of age and was the Commanding Officer of the 11th Armoured Brigade. He is generally regarded as the most outstanding British tank commander of the Second World War.

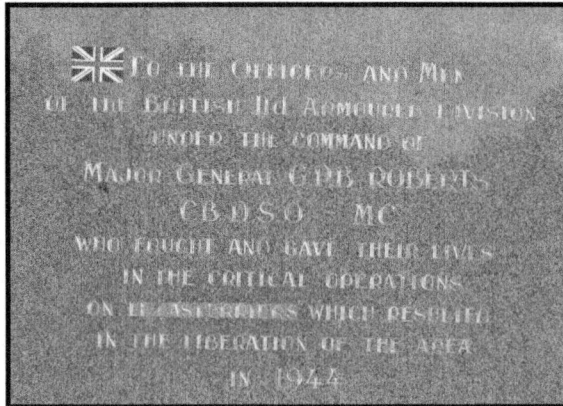

Battle of Le Bas Perrier
Commemorative monument

To put it simply, the Hussars had come down one slope of a valley, liberated a village called Presles at the bottom of the valley, then made their way up the slope on the other side of the valley, and got stuck there. It was typical Normandy scenery, with the usual high hedgerows, banks, and cornfields. They were forced to take up position in on the slope of the hill, with not enough room for the number of tanks they had. Above

them on the ridge of the valley was a village called Chenedolle, from which they were being bombarded by German tanks and artillery. From their own point of view, the Germans were perfectly placed. Their guns could pound the British positions, while keeping just out of range and out of sight of the British tanks. Dad always used to say that the gun they feared most was the 88. The Germans would dig a deep hole and nestle the gun in the hollow, then camouflage it thoroughly. Dad used to say that just one of these gun positions, operated by just half a dozen troops, could hold up the whole regiment for hours, knocking out tanks and firing rounds every two or three seconds.

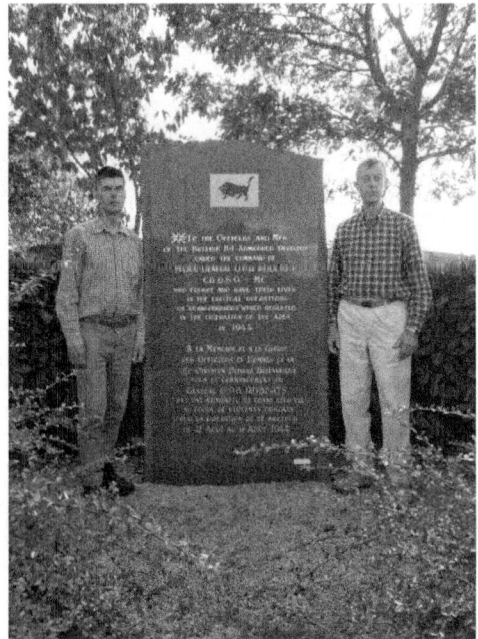

Francis and Edmund at
Le Bas Perrier September 2019

Dad once took us to the Tank Museum at Bovington Camp in Dorset to show us the Sherman and the German tank it was up against, the King Tiger. The Tiger was also equipped with the 88mm gun. Dad explained to us that it did have a vulnerable underbelly at the front, but that just like the moveable artillery gun, the Tiger would be nestled down in a large hole right up to the top of its tracks, with only its strongest body armour above the level of the ground. The Hussars spent five days and nights in these fields, surrounded by the 9th SS Panzer Division. The Battle of Le Bas Perrier even involved hand to hand fighting, but against all the odds, the British managed to hold on to the exposed hillside of Le Bas Perrier, until they were relieved by the advancing British forces. That week saw the loss of 2 officers and 19 other ranks. In addition, over fifty men had been wounded. Dad told us a tragic story that occurred in his unit around this time. The soldiers were always completely exhausted and one night a member of a tank crew could not stay awake and fell asleep. His head crashed down onto a protruding piece of metal which smashed through his temples. He died instantly, seated at his post in the tank.

One day we were holidaying in Normandy and Dad suddenly pulled over and left us all in the car and wandered off through the village we were passing through. He did not explain what he was doing and we were left in the car wondering what was up. When he eventually came back, he explained that he had suddenly recognised clearly that this was a village he had passed through in 1944. He laughingly recalled how he had been proceeding along the road on foot when a group of German soldiers came out in front of him with their guns, only to throw their weapons down and surrender to him. He did not know what to do so he told them to carry on walking along the road in the direction of the advancing British front line.

23rd Hussars emblem carved on the gravestones

Dad loved Normandy very much and was always happy when he was there. In June 1984, when he was 65, the fortieth anniversary of D-Day was celebrated. After the war Dad did not get involved with any regimental associations or reunions of veterans, but that year he did decide to go to Normandy.

He was not part of any official events or celebrations, but one day while he was there, he and Mum were walking along a pavement arm in arm, when a young lady came up to them and spoke to Dad. '*Pardon Monsieur, est-ce que vous avez fait partie de la guerre?*' When Dad said yes, she presented him with a flower and said '*Pour tout ce que vous avez fait pour la France.*'

On the 12th August 1944, the Hussars set out on what was to be the final phase of the Normandy campaign. This was Dad's fourth major battle since landing in Normandy on 15th June. Historians refer to it as The Falaise Pocket. It would last from 12th to 21st August and was to lead to victory in Normandy. That victory meant the end of any serious possibility that the Germans could hold on to France, and thereby signalled the eventual defeat of Germany.

After a slow, steady advance before a retreating German army, the Hussars reached the bridge over the River Roye at Taillebois on 16th August. From there, under very heavy fire, they had to advance on a strongly defended German position on the brow of a hill round the hamlet of Notre Dame de Rocher. Each night, under cover of darkness, the Germans would pull back. As the British pressed forward, they began to see scenes of utter chaos, carnage, and destruction, with smashed vehicles and abandoned hardware everywhere. Dad used to say that one of the most awful things about the war was having to dig a grave and hastily bury a comrade with whom he had been chatting only a little while before. He also said that on the way through the green fields and orchards of Normandy one of the most horrible experiences was the sight of dead cattle and horses, lying abandoned and bloated on the roads and in the fields.

On 18th August 1944, the Hussars once again were chosen to be in the lead, to spearhead the advance of the entire 11th Armoured Division. Dad would have been greatly cheered to know that just six years later, on the same date, his second son Maurice would be born in Cambridge. By 12 noon the group found itself on the high ridge overlooking the river town of Putanges from the west.

Bridge over the River Orne at Putanges

The other side of the river was heavily defended and they could not make the crossing until the following day. The bridge over the Orne at Putanges today bears the name of the 11th Armoured Division. Once they made this all-important river crossing, the British forces were able finally to link up with the American forces, who were sweeping in from west after a very successful operation code-named Cobra. The Germans could not retreat fast enough and found themselves trapped in a vast amphitheatre dictated by the terrain. An incredibly costly and valiant defence was put up by a Polish tank unit which effectively closed off the only German exit route from the encirclement.

Of the entire German Army in Normandy, only 70 tanks managed to escape through the Falaise Gap. 40 German Divisions had been destroyed and a quarter of a million Germans died. The Allies lost 37,000 men, two thirds of whom were British or Canadian. For the 23rd Hussars, the Battle of Normandy had lasted 70 days, or 10 weeks, from 15th June to 24th August. The Hussars suffered 226 casualties, 92 killed and 134 wounded.

Member of the Royal Signals in action in Normandy
Source: Pegasus Museum

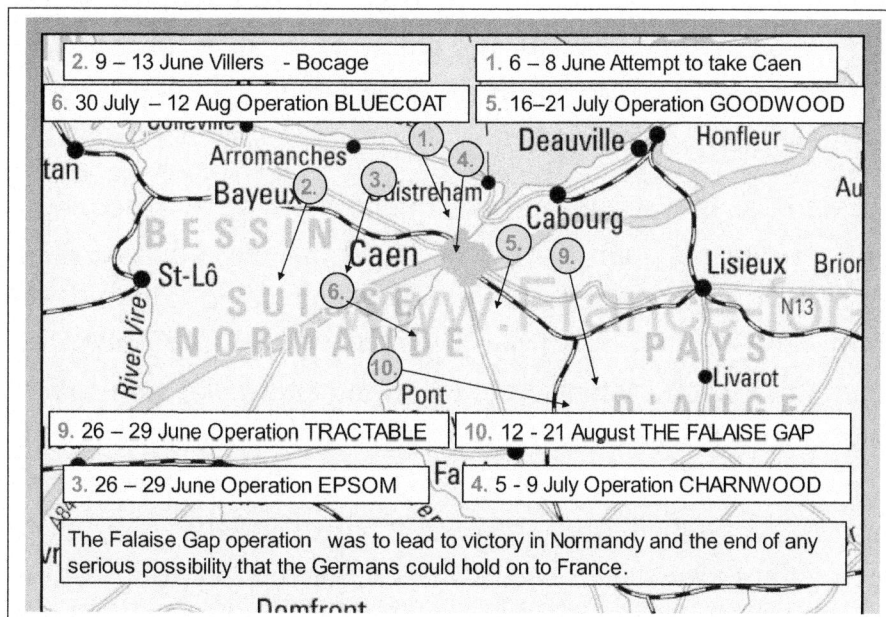

2. 9 – 13 June Villers - Bocage	1. 6 – 8 June Attempt to take Caen
6. 30 July – 12 Aug Operation BLUECOAT	5. 16–21 July Operation GOODWOOD
9. 26 – 29 June Operation TRACTABLE	10. 12 - 21 August THE FALAISE GAP
3. 26 – 29 June Operation EPSOM	4. 5 - 9 July Operation CHARNWOOD

The Falaise Gap operation was to lead to victory in Normandy and the end of any serious possibility that the Germans could hold on to France.

My own summary of the Normandy Campaign in 10 Operations

Chapter 12

Venice

And eight punctures

Without a doubt, Growler's finest hour was the road trip to Venice we made in 1960. There were no motorways, so the journey just to Dover took a whole day. Dad never booked a ferry crossing in his life. He simply turned up and bought a ticket in the squalid little office on the dockside. The only places for refreshment and toilet-stops on our way down through England were Transport Cafes. These were horrendous, filthy, smoke-filled places full of frightening men. They would stare at us when they saw a veteran car pull up alongside the trucks, piled high on the roof and on the rear luggage rack with a ramshackle assortment of sacks and cases and ancient trunks. The cafes were usually adjacent to a petrol station or on wasteland. The buildings were little more than wartime shacks and huts. The toilet facilities were often a single cubicle, with no sign of toilet roll or soap. The air inside was always thick with tobacco smoke, combined with the smell of sausage, bacon, and egg. The only drink on offer was tea. We children were never treated to anything other than a slice of bread and butter or toast.

When we got to Dover and into our queue, by sheer chance we found ourselves parked up alongside John Kerr, who lived in King's Drive. John was the elder brother of Tom Kerr. Although he could not be called Edmund's best friend, Tom was definitely a friend of Edmund. It was thanks to Edmund's friendship with Tom that all of us children used to tag along and make a nuisance of ourselves in the Kerr's beautiful detached King's Drive home. Tom tolerated us younger ones as one might a pack of tame animals. He would sit up on the work surface in his very up-to-date kitchen, open the biscuit barrel and toss biscuits down to us in the style of feeding time at the zoo. Tom's older brother John, whom we were now staring at in the ferry queue at Dover, was a very handsome 20 something, with rich black hair.

His car was a beautiful two-tone Austin Metropolitan, in white below and green above, and with whitewall tyres. John was polite, but not at all amused at the sight of the rabble of Mohan children staring down it him from their embarrassing vehicle. By his side sat an attractive blonde, whom he was careful not to introduce to us.

Outside Omi's flat in Mölheimerstrasse, Freiburg.
Behind: Madeleine, Dad, Omi, Mum, ...?..., Opi, Clemens
In front: Francis, Veronica, Bernadette, Maurice, Edmund

Our crossing was in the middle of the night. This was always Dad's preferred time to cross, since it was the cheapest and ideally gave him an opportunity to snatch some sleep, so that on arrival in France he could forge ahead. The cross-channel ferries in those days were dire, black, and white rust buckets, awash with vomit and urine, with nowhere comfortable to sit. We did not stay together as a family, but were allowed to wander around the boat wherever we wanted. Apart from spark plugs and starting problems, the most common problem with Growler was a puncture.

After the epic journey to Venice and back Dad would proudly relate that he had had eight punctures. In Preston we had a collection of Dad's discarded tyres stored and hidden in the gap between our garage and the garage next door. They made great toys for us children, especially the boys, to play with in the garden and up and down the drive.

What failed, as we drove through the night through Northern France, was the windscreen wiper system. In August 1988, as Dad lay dying in hospital, Edmund and I kept a bedside vigil for several hours. Edmund spoke to Dad and reminded him of that drive through France thirty years earlier, of the night he had driven, for mile upon mile and hour after hour, through the torrential summer storm, with the window wound down and his head stuck out of the window, lashed by rain.

Having fought in the war, Dad believed he could stop anywhere in Europe and do whatever he liked. That was why he drove through the centre of Paris and pulled up under the Arc de Triomphe, where he promptly got out the Calor Gas stove and proceeded to brew up a pot of tea. When the gendarmerie arrived to move him on, Dad disarmed them with his perfect French. I remember being not quite sure whether to feel proud of Dad or embarrassed by him. To get to Italy, Dad chose to drive over the Brenner Pass. As well as being breath-taking, this journey was truly hair-raising. Growler, operating at the limits of his capabilities, crawled and creaked his overloaded body up terrifyingly steep climbs, round hairpin bends and winding cliff-edge roads, with precipitous drops falling away below.

As we motored along, I asked Dad whether it was likely that we would have to drive through cloud. 'I most sincerely hope not,' he replied. I thought how grown-up that sounded and how elegant my father was of speech. As we crawled through the pass, I found that I was the only one of the children awake. My position in the car was in the back corner on the driver's side, behind Veronica. I felt immensely proud and privileged and knew I was taking part in the adventure of a lifetime. Apart from the steady drone of Growler's engine, there was an intense silence ad stillness all around, with no other traffic in sight in either direction. It was late afternoon, early evening. The mountain wall rose above us on our left. A vast valley opened up along our right-hand side, stretching for miles.

A snow-capped mountain range made a wall on the other side of the valley. The sun was fading and reddening the peaks. I went into a trance-like state and felt as if my body was both tiny and enormous at the same time. I was filled with the deepest joy and peace imaginable. I did not need anyone to tell me that God existed. I knew. Everything around me was suffused with intense love and beauty and presence. The experience is as real today as it was then, just as precious as it was on that day when we climbed the alpine pass, the day when only two people were awake, my father and me.

When we crossed the border into Italy, Dad pulled over and got out of the car. When I asked Mum where Dad had gone, she said 'He's just gone to get some money.' I found it very hard to understand how Dad could somehow have these magical deposits of cash all over Europe. I worried that he was not really entitled to get this money and that we could not really afford the holiday.

Dad prided himself on taking us to see many famous sights and places on all his continental holidays. On our way down from the Brenner he made sure that we stopped at the little mountain village of Riese, the birthplace of Pope St Pius X. This was of great significance for Maurice and for me, because of the fact that we attended Pope Pius X school in Preston. We knew that Pius' real name was Giuseppe Sarto and that he had been brought up with a very poor and simple way of life. The house of his birth was a plain, white-washed home with a simple front door. There was a little souvenir shop where I bought a key-ring, which I thought was wonderful. On the end of the key-ring was a little brass book which closed with a very satisfying golden clasp. When you opened it up, out tumbled a concertina of black and white views of the village of Riese and the Sarto home.

Before arriving in Venice, Dad also made sure that we went right into the centre of Padua to see the great basilica of St Antony, the patron saint of our parish church. There I treated myself to another souvenir, a lovely little pen-knife with a shiny red plastic handle. One of the things that always fascinated us boys about the continent was the fact that even at the age of five or six you could go into a shop full of knives and buy one without any questions asked. On a later trip to Germany, I bought a much larger full-scale sheath knife with a five-inch blade. It had a fine real leather sheath through which I could slide my belt, and a decorative faux reindeer horn handle.

Padua was very beautiful and St Antony was like a familiar friend to us because of the statues we had grown up with and because of all the lost or mislaid items he had already found for us, and would continue to find, over the years.

We found a campsite in the tiny Italian fishing village and seaside resort of Chioggia, sitting on the coast and looking out over the lagoon towards Venice. As we arrived Dad steered Growler through the narrowest of ancient streets and nearly got the vehicle completely stuck. The alleyways were crammed with people and full of tiny shops. The locals had never seen anything like this and stopped what they were doing to stand and point and shout and stare. A swarm of local urchins decided to hitch a ride on our car. They clambered onto the already frail running boards on either side of the vehicle and banged on the windows and cheered and jabbered and screamed at the top of their voices, pointing to us children, and laughing at us as if we were exhibits in a zoo.

I cannot remember whether it had any facilities, but we loved the campsite at Chioggia and would remember it fondly for the rest for our lives. It was right on the beach and we seemed to stay there for ever. We could come and go and play all day, completely unsupervised. One evening we went through the local market. There were covered stalls with huge tables piled high with water melons. As we approached, the women who ran the stalls started nudging each other and saying '*inglesi, inglesi*!' Dad was disgusted that they should try to take advantage of us by upping their prices. What the women didn't realise was that we had hardly any money and that Dad certainly was not in the habit of splashing out on random treats for six children.

One thing Dad did find money for was a day trip to Venice. We got up early and travelled by *vaporetto* from Chioggia straight over the lagoon to Venice. We sat down below decks in the beautiful old boat, with its varnished brown wood and brass trimmings. The windows were long and narrow. When we looked out of the windows the water of the lagoon was just below the bottom edge of the windows, while we were seated on wooden benches below sea level.

What a wonderful day it was, as we saw this magical, mythical place come to life before our eyes. The heat was intense. By now our skin was a deep, dark brown. Mum wore a fine yellow sleeveless summer dress. It had a narrow belt and fell in sharp pleats. We bought a paper bag of bird food and held out our arms and hands, which were soon covered in pigeons.

We saw the Bridge of Sighs and the Doge's Palace, the inside of the basilica and the Piazza San Marco, with the enormous column and the lion on top. We were fascinated by the rubbish boats which cruised along the Grand Canal and hoovered up all the rubbish and waste from the mirky waters of the lagoon by catching it in a huge mesh scoop. Alongside the street stalls and kiosks there were displays of pieces of coconut, arranged on tiered supports, which you could buy as a healthy snack. What was fascinating was that water sprinkled down over the coconut pieces to keep them fresh. It would be sixty years before I would return to Venice and when I did, those same little coconut vending stalls were still plying their trade.

It was late afternoon, early evening, when we climbed aboard our river taxi for the long ride across the lagoon to Chioggia. I had a lovely feeling of warmth and tiredness, as the boat glided across the water to take us home to our tent. It was at least two hours and we were all exhausted.

Mum and Dad were very happy. Despite having very little money, they had managed to travel together to the world's most romantic city, even if it was with a gaggle of children in tow. Dad's choice of a camping holiday destination was inspired. Chioggia was an idyllic little fishing village and port, completely unspoilt, built on a spit reaching out towards the lagoon. It had canals and bridges, just like Venice, but on a tiny scale. On the other side of the peninsular from the harbour settlement was the campsite and a beautiful, long beach of perfect sand. The campsites are still there and flourishing at Chioggia today. It was intensely hot at the campsite. One day poor Maurice became very ill. We came back from the beach to find him crying and lying listless inside the shade of the tent. Mum said it was sunstroke. Despite this alarming diagnosis, as far as I know, no form of medical intervention was sought. I found it very upsetting. There did not seem to be any treatment other than rest and staying out of the sun. I had a pair of red swimming trunks which were made of wool. They were very itchy and lumpy and trebled in weight when wet. When I complained Dad told me I was very lucky because the wool dried so quickly in the sun.

The water at the beach was a clear and pure, pale green and sky blue. The sand was a shiny white. There were many Italian couples. The men and their women all had glossy black hair and tanned bodies.

Tourists could hire pedaloes at the beach and paddle around in the calm, still water. The pedaloes were made of wood, not fibreglass or plastic. Maurice and I would wait in the deeper water and then catch hold of the tail ends of a pedaloe and hitch a ride far out to sea. The Italian occupants would scream at us in shrill Italian. The sea was teaming with coloured fish.

Eventually the time came for us to hurl everything back into Growler and head off for the long journey home. After leaving the coast, we stopped to camp at Sirmione, at the southern end of Lake Garda. This was another idyllic location. After pitching tent, Dad took us for our usual stroll to try to tire us out ready for bed. We walked along the lakeside in the evening sun, past the picturesque houses, cafés, and restaurants. We could not pay for anything, or buy anything, but we loved the beauty of this place. Thereafter Mum and Dad would often refer to Sirmione in reverent tones, cherishing it as a wonderful holiday memory. We also had an equally impressive stop at Lake Maggiore, from where we chugged our way slowly back up to the Alps. On one occasion, while travelling at night, we stopped in the square of a little mountain town. A local drunk, ill-shaven and dressed in a dirty grey suit, appeared out of side street, and swayed up to the car, shouting and screaming and shaking his fist at us. Dad explained that he was blaming the English for every misfortune brought upon Italy by the Second World War. After Maggiore, Growler chugged his way via Bergamo, Como, and Lugano, to make the homeward journey along the 2000m high St Gotthard Pass. We camped overnight at Andermatt in Switzerland. Both Mum and Dad thought this was wonderful, but it was 1400 metres above sea level and even in the summer we were freezing at night. We thought it was very bleak indeed, especially after the beauty and warmth of the Veneto and the lakes.

Wherever we went, we never seemed to have enough money to do the things that normal people did, such as have a drink or a snack or a meal in a café. On our way through France, we stopped at a small restaurant with white walls and simple white tables. Dad ordered a bowl of frog's legs, *les cuisses de grenouilles*, for Mum and we all sat round staring at her while she ate them. I don't remember us having anything at all. When a grumpy waitress came in with the dish, Mum cried out '*ooh là là!*' when she saw them, just to get into the mood for being in France.

Dad liked to do things to extremes. He specialised in driving endlessly for hour after hour. When he was tired, he would simply pull Growler over to the side of the road, wrap himself in a blanket and roll into a ditch, where he would fall instantly asleep.

At home us boys would play a game of pretending to be Dad doing this. We would take it turns to sit on a chair and pretend to be driving, and then make as if to steer suddenly and violently off the road and roll seamlessly out of the door into a heap on the floor, while wrapping a blanket round us in one smooth action, While Dad slept, we would all have to wait in silence for an hour or so. We were not allowed to open the car doors in case this woke Dad. His ability to switch off and go unconscious had been learned in his army days, when snatching opportunities for sleep had been essential.

Dad loved to be away on the continent for the whole of the summer. He loved to get away from Britain, the British people, and the British way of life. One thing that depressed him above all things was when he had to camp on the way home, usually somewhere not that far from the Channel, and the campsite would be full of English people on their way back to Blighty. As he shaved in the facilities, his fellow countrymen would greet him with a cheery 'Morning!' and engage him in conversation. Behind the camaraderie was a sense that they were the only ones who knew when to get up and how to shave and that soon they would be able to leave Johnny Foreigner behind. Dad hated this breaking of the spell of his summer escape. His stomach would turn over with the dread of the return to work.

Dad was very forgetful and did lots of stupid things. Unfortunately, I would inherit this characteristic. One of the worst things Dad did was on the way back from the Venice holiday, when he managed to lose the passports. This happened on the way home, after a night-time drive through Belgium. Dad simply presented himself at the British Consulate in Calais in order to obtain the papers that would allow him and his family to be repatriated. Growler was parked up in a side street and we all sat for what seemed like hours, not knowing what was going to happen. At one point an attractive woman with sophisticated make-up and a blonde beehive hair-do and wearing a smart blue two-piece suit appeared at the window of the car and spent some time peering in. She was trying to count us to see if Dad's story was true and perhaps to see if we really did look like British citizens. This story had an epilogue. Years later, and I do not know how many years it was, a parcel arrived in the post. Inside were the passports, now long out of date. It turned out that Dad had left them behind in his portmanteau of documents in a dingy all-night cafe / bar in Belgium, where he had stopped for a midnight dose of refreshment in the middle of one of his all-night treks. The cafe had eventually changed hands and the new proprietor had found the briefcase and documents stuffed away in the corner of a cupboard underneath the counter.

Chapter 13

Freiburg im Breisgau

And Kaffe und Kuchen

O ur journey to Venice started and ended at our grandparents' flat in Freiburg, a heavenly place for us and a home from home. A common pattern of our continental camping holidays was to cross from Dover and then head straight for Omi's flat. This tended to be a hell-for-leather drive across Northern France, using the *Route Nationale* through Reims and Châlons-sur-Marne (now rebranded as Châlons-en-Champagne!) then east to Metz and into Germany at Strasbourg. Châlons-sur-Marne became Dad's watchword for milk that had gone off. Once, when camping at Châlons, I went with Dad to get some milk from the local dairy. A grubby farmer with a *Gauloise* hanging out of the corner of his mouth went to a dirty bucket that sat on the floor in the corner of the barn, stirred it up a bit with a ladle and scooped it into a glass bottle. Alternatively, Dad would head straight through the night on the floodlit Belgian motorway system, camp overnight in Aachen, and then get down to Freiburg in one big trek down the free German Autobahn system.

On our visits to Omi we always seem to arrive at *Mülheimerstrasse* late at night. We come off the autobahn and follow the main road into Freiburg from the West, the *Basler Landstrasse.* We buzz the bell at the main entrance at the bottom, and then push the door as Omi releases it in response. To us this is very advanced engineering. As soon as we start to climb the cold stone staircase the lights come on automatically. More amazing technology. Our nostrils fill with the smell of German cement and paint. Omi lives on the second floor on the right-hand side. She comes out and stands in the doorway on the landing. She is laughing and crying with the excitement and joy of seeing us all again. She names each one of us in turn as we troop into the flat, bleary-eyed, and weary from our travelling. Omi strokes our cheeks and hair and tells us how fine and beautiful we look. We will bed down in her little flat for the night and move on the next morning to set up camp at the municipal campsite.

Dad loved speaking German and enjoyed Omi and Opi's company. He would enjoy telling Omi stories about the journey. She would laugh and giggle and put her hand over her mouth and look around amused and worried, with a glint in her eye. Dad would call Opi *Vädelchen*, Little Father, and would enjoy a cigar and a *schnapps* with him. Opi always insisted that the brandy be downed in one. Dad did not like to stay in the flat for long. He started to feel boxed in and restless and wanted to return to the freedom of the municipal campsite, and then on to the next leg of the trip, his real holiday. Besides, in the flat, Uncle Clemens would drive him mad. Clemens did not go in for genuine conversation. Instead, he bellowed out *non sequiturs* and a barrage of acerbic comments that required no response. He was extremely genial and exuded an almost overbearing friendliness alongside an old-fashioned courtesy. He was restless and easily bored or distracted. He liked to annoy Dad with little challenges and niggling asides. He always insisted that Dad share the vast supply of *Ganterbräu* he kept in the family *Keller* in the basement of the building, which Dad did, but more out of duty than any real interest.

On the municipal campsite we would take our time in the morning over a leisurely breakfast, without a doubt Dad's favourite meal of the day throughout his life. Dad would send one of us to the little wooden hut where we could ask for *zehn Brötchen bitte*, the delicious German breakfast rolls.

One of our ideas of heaven was the Schwarzwald and the Schauinsland. We knew that Schauinsland meant 'look into the land.' Standing on his tiny balcony at the back of the *Mülheimerstrasse*, Opi would point up to the Schauinsland and tell Dad to admire the *schönes Panorama*. From the centre of Freiburg, it was possible to get a sleek yellow tram to the outskirts of the city, from where you could take the red cable car all the way to the summit of this beautiful mountain and look across the Rhine valley to the Vosges. When he was little, Edmund would sit with a wooden coffee bean grinder and pretend that he was driving a German tram. Of course, we never took the cable car as we could never have afforded it. Dad enjoyed driving up the hairpin bends and pulling in at a random bit of grassy hillside. We would disgorge and go on foot on a forest *Wanderung*, fragrant with the scent of pine in the summer heat. In the summer a Sportscar or *Rennwagen* hill climb event would take place on the Schauinsland, with the cars starting in Freiburg.

One summer Dad took us to see it. Needless to say, we did not pay for entry to any official enclosure or viewing point. We climbed up the hillside on forest paths and paused by the bends in the roads to watch the racing cars roar past, just a few feet away. As we were returning down the mountain to get back to the car, we lost track of Edmund, who was always very self-confident and ambitious and liked to forge ahead. He was probably also keen to free himself from any association with the rabble of his family. Dad was very worried and started to shout 'Edmund!' Immediately from somewhere in the trees came the mocking mimicry of a group of Germans echoing Dad's cry of 'Edmund!' Dad went mad at this and let loose a torrent of invective in fluent German.

As avid readers of the Victor, and children of a former soldier, we were imbued with the idea that we had won the war and that Germany had been heavily bombed and defeated. When we travelled to Germany in 1960, we left behind a Britain that was still scarred by bomb damage and struggling to build a new country in the post-war world. Upon arrival in Germany, just 15 years after the war, we found ourselves in a prosperous country, immaculately clean and perfectly rebuilt, with barely a scrap of evidence of the trauma of the 1940s.

Freiburg was a city of immense beauty. It was dominated by its cathedral, the famous Freiburger Münster, or Cathedral of Our Lady. Unaltered since 1330, the Münster had miraculously survived the allied raid of November 1944, despite the entire square and market all around it being destroyed. The spire consisted of a unique filigree of hollow tracery which rose over a hundred metres into the air and was set against the Black Forest hillsides surrounding the town.

The *Münsterplatz* was the heart of the town and still boasted a beautifully reconstructed medieval *Rathaus* and other medieval buildings and colonnades. Another iconic survivor from the medieval period was the *Martinstor*, a huge Gothic gateway formerly set in the medieval city walls. In reconstructing the city after the war, the Germans had preserved the ancient street plan. This meant that the whole town still had the intimacy and historic ambience of its former days. The river flowing through the city was called the *Dreisam* and we would pass over it on our way between Omi's and the camp site. It had a translucent pale green colour and passed over a cobbled channel in terraced steps. Magically, the crystal clear waters of the *Dreisam* flowed through the streets of the town in little runnels or *Bächle*. These miniature streams, running down the centre or sides of the streets and refreshing the air in the summer, dated all the way back to the 12th century.

The main department store in Freiburg was called Hertie. Whenever we came back from a visit to the town centre, Opi, himself a former shopkeeper, would be very keen to know whether we had been to Hertie or not. For Sunday Mass we would go to the *Johanneskirche*. This was a vast red sandstone building which you got to before you arrived at the city centre. The first five or six pews of the church would be filled exclusively with elderly women in widow's black. They would wail the hymns in a tragic chorus. The priests would enunciate the liturgy in perfect tones, *Herr, ebarme dich unser*. We would try to be in Freiburg for Omi's birthday on the 21st August. In 1960 Omi was 67 years old, but very alert and sprightly. For her birthday, a coven of very elderly women would gather at the flat for *Kaffee und Kuchen*. These were the *Blubber Tante*. Dressed entirely in Edwardian black dresses, which reached right to the ground, these exiles from their beloved homeland would chatter and grumble in dark tones as they tucked into their coffee and cake.

Kaffee und Kuchen, with the rich aroma of coffee and the delicious smell of fresh-baked cake, encapsulated the German experience of home, of *Gemütlichkeit*. Coffee would never taste as good as this, and nor would cake. A cup of tea at home might be perfect for a slice of Victoria Sandwich or Lemon Drizzle. But only rich black coffee could do justice to the yeast and almond taste of Omi's *Streuselkuchen*, or her fruity *Zwetschgen* cake, topped with lashings of sweet *Schlagsahne*.

Abendbrot at Omi's was a simple meal, a slice of *Roggenbrot*, *Tilsiterkäse*, tomatoes and *Schinken*. As we sat on Omi's couch in a row, our tea would be set out on the coffee table, As we munched, we would watch the news on the *Zweites Deutsches Fernsehen* channel. Behind us the beautiful face of Martha Bucholz, Omi's mother, gazed down upon us from a gilt framed oil painting.

As an alternative to the depressing *Johanneskirche*, we would sometimes attend Mass at Sankt Georgen, a settlement on the *Baslerlandstrasse* as you went out of town towards the autobahn. This was a very pleasant modern church with a friendly approach to the liturgy. The interior was pure white, except for an elaborate carved and painted reredos behind the altar.

When visiting Freiburg one of the greatest treats was a visit to the *Erlenbacher Hütte* in Oberried. Throughout the Black Forest, high up in the hills, were little forest huts or café restaurants called *Hütte*. To visit a *Hütte* was Uncle Clemens' greatest joy in life and the *Erlenbacher Hütte* was his favourite.

He would drive us up the steep mountain roads in his VW Beetle. Inside the tiny restaurant he would make himself known to all and sundry as if he was a long-lost son returning to his home. He would order a selection of *wurst* and *schinken*, served on a wooden board, with horseradish sauce and *Kartoffelsalat* washed down with a *Ganterbräu*. Clemens would flirt with the waitress, especially if she was under the age of 40 and wearing the Bavarian *dirndl* dress. '*Da kann Mann gut verheiraten*,' was the wistful comment delivered by Clemens after an exchange with the waitress, which always struck us as somewhat incongruous, given that Clemens never had any intention to marry. Any car journey with Clemens was painfully embarrassing, as he insisted on eyeing up any female on the pavement or in a nearby vehicle, hitting us on the arm and shouting 'A girl for you Eddy!' or 'A girl for you Nany!'

Clemens' bedroom was immediately on the left as you entered Omi's flat. We thought it was very glamorous because it was decorated with posters of Spanish bullfights. Spain and Majorca were Uncle Clemens' holiday destination of choice. From the main living room, we could step out onto the tiny balcony with its corrugated iron sides. Omi and Opi's bedroom lay beyond the dining / living room. The flat was entered by means of a small lobby and immediately on the right was the toilet. We always found the toilet hilarious because it had a large inspection platform, which would be the first destination for one's waste, prior to its onward journey. This allowed the Germans to conduct a daily audit of the health of their bowels. The flush was a small metal lever which could only be operated if it was pressed down very hard. This would release a high-pressure torrent, which would shoot the deposits off the inspection ledge. Speaking of bowels, *Durchfall*, the German for diarrhoea, was a word much in use in Freiburg, especially when we had been forced to consume just one too many bowlfuls of the dreaded *Mirabellen* plums.

If you carried on past the toilet you came to the little galley kitchen, and then from there into the bathroom, which had a sink, a bath, and an Ascot-style water heater. Opi was known for the lengthy raspberries he emitted as he shuffled round the flat. We boys found it very amusing to play at being Opi, blowing through our lips and pretending to be jet-propelled through the flat.

To stop ourselves going mad in Omi's tiny apartment we would spend all our free time on the *Spielplatz*. Omi's block of flats was one of about a dozen blocks, all hastily erected after the war with help from the Americans. The buildings themselves, and the apartments they contained, were simple to the point of being quite primitive, but they were generously planned around a large green park, at the centre of which lay the play area. The principal piece of equipment was the *Rundlauf*, a device I have never encountered anywhere else. It was a sort of maypole, with about six chains hanging down from the rotating disc at the top. At the end of the chains were what looked like little sections of ladder, with the four rungs made of wood but joined vertically by chain. If you were not very tall you would use the lowest rung; if you were taller you used the higher rungs. Ideally, you could place both your hands on different rungs. You then scooted round and round, flying through the air and wacking your feet on the ground every so often to boost your speed. It was very dangerous, because every time someone gave up, they would leave their chains and wooden bars flailing around and these could easily hit you in the face. At the *Rundlauf* we would meet up with all the local children and it was there that we made friends with a young American lad whose father was in the occupying forces. He was very over-confident and knew everything that there was to know.

The flats had been built on a green field site and in the early days they backed onto a huge area of fields in which sweetcorn was grown. One day we three boys were bored so we went on a little trek along the gravel paths between the sweetcorn. We came upon an old bus which had been parked up on one of these agricultural tracks and looked as if it had been abandoned. We decided to have a bit of fun and let the air out of the tyres. Unfortunately, an aggressive man of military bearing suddenly appeared and caught us in the act. When Maurice and I detected the word *Polizei* in the torrent of invective, we lost all our bravado and burst into tears. Edmund was much more composed and somehow extricated us from the situation, from which there were no further repercussions. When Edmund related this incident to our American friend, he did so with his usual air of calm detachment. We did not tell our parents.

Above Omi's flat, on the third floor, lived Frau Karcher and her partner Herr Bührer. They exuded Bavarian friendliness. They were both short and round and well built. They were always laughing and joking and both of them spoke with booming voices. They were very welcoming and we would often bed down in their flat. Frau Karcher had short blonde hair, Herr Bührer had sleek black hair and an unshaven look.

They had a rather dapper son called Günther, who was already in his twenties and only seemed to make fleeting appearances. Their daughter Ingrid was also in her twenties and was very much the epitome of the sixties, with blonde bob, tanned skin, and trendy clothes. During the Venice expedition Growler developed a problem whereby the car battery would become dislodged from its bracket. Herr Bührer was very good at welding and made Dad a custom-built housing to keep the battery secure for the journey home.

Not far outside Freiburg, on the road to Kirchzarten and the Black Forest, was a suburb called Littenweiler, which had an open-air swimming pool or *Strandbad*. This always seemed like another world of prosperity and peace. There were four large stone sculptures of lions, one on each corner. The huge pool was surrounded by lawns and trees. The teenage girls and boys were tanned and lithe in their sporty bathing costumes. They slid through the waters like seals, and laughed confidently as they played ball games around the pool. They were like creatures from another planet. I wanted to be part of this perfect world, but knew that I was out of place. As the local girls cavorted, with smooth skin and honey coloured hair, I floundered in the water, or skulked on the grass like a feeble slug.

If you carried on past Littenweiler and into the Schwarzwald, the road passed through the narrow gorge of the Höllental. Here we would look up to catch a glimpse of the *Hirschsprung*. High up on one side of the craggy cliff stood the imposing statue of a stag, looking across the narrow top of the gorge. This was to commemorate the legendary incident when a stag had been chased through the forest by a knight from the nearby Falkenstein castle. When the stag come to the gorge, it made a heroic leap across the gap to escape its pursuer.

Each time we went to Omi's, when the time came to leave, she would give each of us a *Beutelchen* or small bag. This was a little plastic pull string bag, with coloured patterns on the see-through cellophane. She would pass it through the windows of Growler, as we took our places for the long journey home. Her slender frame would be standing at the entrance to the flats, with tears running down her cheeks as she waved us off. We would soon be examining our sweet bags to check the contents out. We would then play a game, which was to see who could make their *Beutelchen* last the longest. Often the contents were praline chocolates, which would get sat upon, or would melt in the heat of the car.

Titisee - a favourite destination for a day out from Freiburg

Dad relaxing in his army shorts and sandals

Chapter 14

Neckarsteinach

And a girl called Anemone

Our first camping trip to Loch Lomond took place in 1958, when I was six. Our epic trip to Venice was in 1960, when I was eight. It was hard to imagine that this experience could be bettered, but the following year, in 1961, when I was nine, we travelled over to Germany for what was undoubtedly one of greatest events of our childhood, the wedding of Uncle Günther. The wedding took place in the beautiful riverside settlement of Neckarsteinach. This gorgeous place seemed to be the very epitome of the peaceful, settled, rural Germany we loved so much. The little town sat on a sweeping bend of the River Neckar, about ten miles upstream of the iconic city of Heidelberg. Neckarsteinach, which boasted four castles, was nestled on the northern bank of the river Neckar, and belonged to the land of Hesse. Our campsite, somewhat impractically, was situated on the southern side of the river in the lea of a hill called the Dilsberg. The campsite was called *Campingplatz unter'm Dilsberg*. It was reached via a winding lane and was situated on a narrow strip of flat land alongside the river. On the river was a non-stop parade of river traffic in both directions, huge barges and cruisers passing by the campsite all day long. The barges would have little gardens on them, and cars, and dogs, and washing flying in the breeze. On the edge of the river was a pontoon and we boys would spend happy hours standing on this short floating jetty. It was highly hazardous, but Dad never commented or issued any warnings at all.

Uncle Günther's bride was a beautiful young woman called Hedwig Debo. Before making our way to Neckarsteinach, we made our usual first stopover in Freiburg with Omi and Opi. Günther and Hedwig came down from Heidelberg to see us and to introduce Hedwig before the wedding. She was very quiet and shy and impossibly slim. She was dressed very smartly in a pale lilac two-piece outfit. We were fascinated by her white stiletto-heeled shoes and could not believe that she could walk on them.

The wedding day started with the nuptial Mass at the *Herz Jesu* church in Neckarsteinach, the town's Catholic Parish Church. Maurice and I were given the great honour of serving at the Mass, by special request of Uncle Günther. This meant that we were very close to the bride and groom throughout the whole wedding ceremony. The *Herz Jesu Kirche*, or Sacred Heart Church, was a perfect baroque chapel with a beautifully decorated interior in the German / Austrian style. It had clean, white walls on the outside, with the corners and the classical doorway picked out in a lovely red sandstone. The chapel was situated on the right of a gently sloping road called the *Kirchenstrasse*, which led up through the town from the river. The entrance had huge ancient wooden carved doors on very large hinges. In front of the baroque façade was a wide-open space or forecourt. Maurice was just coming up to his tenth birthday and I had turned nine in April. We reported for duty early at the church to be fitted out with crisp white cottas. Our cassocks were bright green, something unheard of in England. There were other local altar servers, who were all older than us; they treated us with authoritative disdain and did not let us do the bell, cruets, or thurible. At the time of communion, the altar server next to me whispered '*Geh mit deinem Brüder!*' but for some reason or other, and typical of me, I went to the wrong side at the wrong time and ended up not receiving Holy Communion. This was upsetting; I had never before been to Mass and not received communion. It was such an important occasion and I felt as if I had let everybody down.

The wedding reception was held in the village in a large square room on the first floor of an elegant old *Gasthaus*, with windows looking out over the river valley. Hedwig looked very beautiful. She was so slim and had such elegant features. Her striking auburn hair was cut short in the sixties style. Her wedding dress was simple and stylish. The bride and groom sat on the traditional top table. During the meal Uncle Günther called me over to him and put his arm round me and said that he had heard that I had not managed to have Holy Communion. Günther had a beautiful kindly face, with a high forehead on which there was a scar from the war. His rich black hair was swept back from his forehead. Günther treated me with great care. He was not disappointed and was not telling me off. He was genuinely upset for me and did not want to embarrass me. He just wanted me to know that he knew and that it was fine.

One of the highlights of the wedding reception was *Apfelsaft*. We could not believe our luck when we were told that we could simply go up to the bar and ask for *Ein Apfelsaft bitte* and a *dirndl*-clad beauty behind the bar would promptly pour it for us. We had never experienced anything like this and we all proceeded to down pints of apple juice. The bonus was that this was top quality apple juice. At Omi's flat, Opi would give us *Apfelsaft* diluted with water, which we thought was disgusting.

The most memorable moment of the wedding reception was our family rendition of *Who Killed Cock Robin?* German weddings are occasions for mini-talent shows and for this one and only occasion the collective Mohan family rose to the challenge and sang our way through all thirteen verses, led by Dad who fortunately knew all the lyrics. It was certainly a grim and bizarre choice for a wedding. Madeleine was just under three years old at the time. For the wedding she wore her famous strawberry dress, a white dress with strawberries on it in relief. We would go up to her and ask her for a strawberry and pretend to pinch it off her dress and eat it, while she screamed in indignation. She would have been too young to join in the song, so it would have been us five older children who formed the Von Trapp-style choir. The song went down brilliantly with the Germans, who loved hearing the English doing their eccentric singing. I was very proud of Dad for singing out in his very fine voice and for knowing all the words, and very pleased for all of us for being able to perform in public.

However, the real highlight of the wedding was Anemone, a beautiful relative of the Rohfleisch family. Anemone must have been in her twenties. She was beautiful, with lustrous black hair, gorgeous laughing eyes, and a lovely slim and sprightly figure. Anemone was very kind to all of us children. She did not dismiss us, but chatted to us all and got to know us and laughed all the time she was with us. Being with her was like being bathed in sunshine and happiness. We had never seen or met a creature as fun and feminine as her, and we never would again. She had a sister or cousin with her called Gundula. Gundula wore a powder blue organza creation with scalloped bows or swathes round the lower edge of the skirt. We called her 'Gundula Gas Bag' and said that her dress was like a Zeppelin airship and the festoons around the skirt were for hanging on to in case she took off and floated away. After that day, we never saw Anemone again.

Outside Mülheimerstrasse 33

Preparing to leave Omi and Opi's for the journey home

Bernadette with her head sticking out, Dad at the wheel, Mum in the passenger seat, Madeleine on Mum's lap, Edmund on the mudguard, Maurice and Francis with sun visors.

Omi would join her hands together whenever she was anxious.

Opi always wore a dark suit and liked to stay on the sidelines.

Chapter 15

More King's Drive moments and memories

And Carola Hinz

When we were little we had scooters and tricycles, but as we got older, we all got beautiful new bicycles. Mine was a very fine bright blue Raleigh. The day we received our first bicycle of our own was a very special day indeed. Despite the demands on his time, Dad took it on himself to teach me to ride a bike. This meant coming out with me in the early evening after tea and taking me 'round the block', He held firmly with his right hand underneath my saddle and I pedalled away. We went up King's Drive to the Garstang Road, then turned left in the northerly direction to go up the Garstang Road away from Preston and up past the Esso garage. We then turned left into Black Bull Lane, which brought us back round to the Corner and then left into King's Drive. I loved this special time on my own with my Dad all to myself and felt very special and important. I think we only did the practices two or three times. Dad was secretly removing his hand and letting me cycle on my own without knowing. I could not believe it when we got back home and he told me that he had not actually been holding on to the saddle at all. I could ride a bike!

Dad always had an eye out for a bargain. At one point they were getting rid of some old furniture from the Little Sisters of the Poor on the Garstang Road. Dad became the proud owner of a very large pine sideboard, which he quickly painted in grey gloss to make it look more modern and to match the morning room furniture. He also got a set of wooden stools which he also painted in a glossy grey. Above the grey sideboard there were wall cupboards with sliding doors. In these wall cupboards at the left-hand end were kept the ingredients for a Mixture. It was Veronica who taught me how to make my first Mixture in a tea cup. A Mixture consisted of cocoa powder, oats, sugar, and evaporated milk. It was used as a remedy for mid-morning or mid-afternoon hunger or boredom. We were not allowed to make them, which made them even more fun and delicious.

Mum's afternoon naps were the ideal opportunity to make a secret Mixture. In the cupboard, next to the oats and sugar, you could also find Instant Whip, as well as Cremona, which was a powder which could be made into a fizzy drink. There was also a packet of desiccated coconut, which was ideal for sprinkling on top of strawberry or even caramel Instant Whip.

Edmund, the eldest, was very good at organising games. The dining table in the dining room slid apart so that you could put a leaf in it. Edmund turned this into a Sherman tank, with a broom serving as the cannon. The tank commander, of course, was Edmund. His head and shoulders stood out above the gap in the table. Maurice was the driver and I was the gunner, both of us squatting on the floor below. Edmund named this tank *Endeavour*.

We would make a lot of mess when we played. One afternoon Mum told us that we had to tidy the dining room up. Edmund devised a simple and logical system. Everything in the room was put in a heap in the middle of the room. Edmund sat in a chair and directed operations. The rest of us had to pick up an object and show it to Edmund. He would then give us clear instructions as to where it was supposed to go.

It might be hard to imagine it now, but sometimes we boys played Mass. This involved setting up a mock altar, with candles a plate and cup, dressing Edmund in a make-shift chasuble and stole, and Maurice and I serving as altar boys. We would offer him faux cruets, bowl, and serviette, and holding onto the corners of his vestments as he knelt before holding up the host. We knew the Latin prayers off by heart.

Mum had a wooden clothes-horse, which could be set up on the lawn to make a perfect frame for a tent. We would then drape it with an old brown army surplus blanket. Once we all draped army blankets over our shoulders and wandered round the garden in a little group, pretending to be the Israelites in the desert. Edmund played the part of Moses and led us round, and when he said 'And there they camped,' we all had to instantly drop down on the grass screaming with laughter. And when he said 'And so they moved on for three days and three nights,' we would all have to stand up together and trudge behind Edmund to another part of the garden.

One day a door-to-door request was made in King's Drive for toys for underprivileged and handicapped children. Mum impressed on us the importance of being generous and charitable. From our own personal toy collection, we all gave up something precious such as a cherished toy car or doll. Eventually it came out that the whole scheme had been a scam and the toys had simply been sold on for profit. Mum stood on the front doorstep and spoke at length to one of the neighbours. 'Everyone of them made a genuine sacrifice' she said, disgusted at the fraud, but very proud of her children.

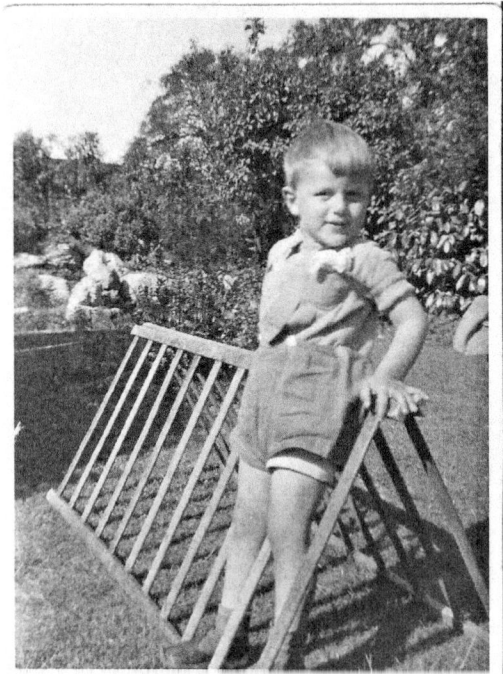

In the garden at King's Drive with the wooden clothes horse

One of Mum's best friends in Preston was a fellow resident of King's Drive. Josie Noblett lived on the other side of the road, further up in the Garstang Road direction, but before you got to Eastgate. Josie's husband Frank was a butcher and they had one child, a quiet and well-behaved daughter called Barbara. Frank and Barbara were both very quiet and I think we thought they were rather on the dull side. Barbara did not go to Winckley Square but to its rival, Lark Hill. Lark Hill was another Catholic convent school, run by the Faithful Companions of Jesus. It had been housed in Victorian times in a Georgian mansion to which a convent and school building had been added.

It regarded itself as a cut above the Convent of the Holy Child Jesus at Winckley Square. Josie was the opposite of dull. She was bursting with life and laughter and loved to be in Mum's company. She and Mum used to meet up for coffee at the Kardomah in Preston. They would speak in hushed and conspiratorial tones of this venue that was the epitome of modernity. The premises were in Fishergate and the eight letters of the coffee shop's title were set out in a mid-century font with each of the letters sitting inside its own square panel.

Much of our free time in King's Drive was spent on our bikes. We would cycle up and down and around King's Drive, Queen's Drive, Westgate, Eastgate and Regent's Drive, without ever venturing out onto the Garstang Road or Black Bull Lane. Often, we would make a nuisance of ourselves by placing a strip of cardboard around a spoke and turning our pushbikes into motor cycles. This produced a very loud noise just like a motorbike. Often our bikes were horses and we would play at shooting each other under the crossbar and through the gap, just like the cowboys did in the Westerns. We used to practise arriving at the side of the house or at the front gate and parking the bike deftly by sliding off it in one quick motion, in imitation of the cowboys arriving at the horizontal wooden bar outside the saloon. We even tried attaching ropes to our handlebars so that we could turn them into reins. A lot of our time was spent riding our bikes no hands, as this was regarded as an admirable and even essential skill. Dad taught each one of us the basics of bicycle maintenance. We had little leather pouches attached to the two metal loops at the back of our saddles and these contained the essential spanner, the tyre brace for hooking into the spokes and removing the outer tyre and a puncture repair kit for the inner tube. Dad taught us how to remove the cotter pin on the pedal crank shaft, how to change and adjust the brake pads and how to oil the chain, as well as how to remove and replace the inner tube and how to find a puncture using a washing up bowl of water. Sometimes we would ask Mum for a Brillo pad and would clean off the little spots of rust accumulating on the chrome and the wheel.

One day there was a ring on the front door bell and we opened the front door to find a policeman on either side of a slim young lady with a bob of mousy hair and a cardigan and pencil skirt. The girl pointed to her mouth to show that she had lost her voice. The policemen explained that she had turned up at the police station in Preston and asked them to help her to find the Mohan family.

This was Carola Hinz, a German girl or young lady who might have been some sort of distant relation from East Prussia. How she could travel all the way from Germany without my parents expecting her and without knowing their address was a mystery to us all. She stayed with us for a long time and it was lovely to have a German with us and to hear the German language spoken. At the same time, we children did find her somewhat humourless and did not take her too seriously.

One of Carola Hinz's comments was that when she listened to English pop music all she heard was 'a horrible noise.' We did not in fact have much exposure to the 'Hit Parade' in Preston, but we were certainly aware of Lonny Donegan, because of the songs 'Does your Chewing Gum lose its Flavour on the Bedpost Overnight' and 'My Old Man's a Dustman.' We also knew about Tommy Steele and when we went round to Tom Kerr's house, we would sometimes ask him if we could go into the lounge and put a record on the record player. Our favourite was Little White Bull, which was on a Decca album called Tommy the Toreador. On the cover of was a cartoon-style bull fight scene featuring Tommy Steele's face superimposed on the figure of a bull fighter.

An essential accessory for our boys' games was the cap gun, of which we always had several in working condition. These were of varying quality and I do not think we could afford better models. The real standard was the Colt 45, with a long zinc alloy barrel and white plastic 'bone' finishing on the handle. We could go to Mrs Corbett's to get the caps in a roll of 50 or 100 shots and would buy several packets at once in little circular containers. It was always good to know that you had a spare cap roll in your pocket. Some of our friends had cowboy hats and outfits, but the most we had were holsters. This meant we could have quick-on-the-draw contests and cycle round with our guns at our side. We also enjoyed loading the caps and then swinging the barrel up into position with a flick of the wrist. We would use our left hand to fire the gun by palming back our hand over the hammer. The smell and sound and spark of the gunpowder exploding with a puff of smoke was intoxicating.

Perhaps our favourite weapon, especially as we got a bit older, was the Spud Gun. We three boys each invested in an identical model in powder-coated shiny blue metal, with a red plastic cover on the end of the barrel. We would set up Special Forces style scenarios where we had to creep around the back or front of the house with our gun at eye level, held by both hands, hoping to catch each other out and send a stinging pellet of potato onto someone's cheek.

The only household pet we had in Preston was a budgerigar named Peterkin. Peterkin was a beautiful green in colour and an extremely friendly and cheeky character. When Mum was peeling potatoes, she loved to let Peterkin out of his cage. He would then sit on the side of the bowl she was using and nibble away at any potato peelings he could find. *'Trill Makes Budgies Bounce with Health'* was the slogan used on the TV ad for the birdseed on which Peterkin was fed. He loved to have the freedom of the house and would hop onto our heads, going from one child to another. Sadly, one day the inevitable happened. Someone left the kitchen door open and Peterkin took his chance to escape. It was impossible to get him back and we felt very sorry for him having to fend for himself out in the unknown.

The most important recreational item in the lives of us boys, and an essential part of 1950s street life, was the trolley. We were fortunate in having Edmund who was a natural engineer and designer. He put our trolley together using old pram wheels, probably from Madeleine's pram once she had out grown it. The smaller wheels were placed at the front with a swivelling bar of wood above. You put your feet on this bar of wood to steer, but we also had a rope attached on each side of the bar to use as a steering rein. We would take it in turns to push each other up to speed. The trolley was in constant need of repair but we were very proud of having one and there were never any parental restrictions on its use or abuse.

While teaching at Preston Catholic College, Dad ran an annual trip to Germany. He would always come back with some nice presents for us children. After one of his trips Dad brought back a German glue-together railway station kit. We did not have a train set but this did not matter. German toys were always beautifully made, Märklin producing products far superior to Hornby. The railway station was called *Zindelstein* and on one evening Mum sat down at the black shiny table in the morning room and made the railway station. It took a long time. Mum sat at the kitchen end of the table and I stood next to her watching her intently and learning how to follow the instructions and assemble the kit. My brothers and sisters sat round the table, watching while they played and read. I needed to do a poo but did not want to leave the proceedings. Mum kept telling me that she could smell something and did I need to go to the toilet. I stubbornly kept on saying 'No, I'm fine,' and ended up doing a poo in my trousers.

Throughout my early years, I suffered from nightmares of fighting in the war. I was always a German soldier, not a British one. I would be defending a position and would always have to retreat in the end. These dreams were very real and frightening. I did not tell anyone about them. There was one recurring nightmare which was even more disturbing, a dream which is impossible to describe. This dream or vision is of an amorphous blob or shape. It is like a haggis or a bladder. It is a sort of ovoid sac. It is not alive, but it is alive. It is grey in colour, but it has no colour. It does not make a sound, but it radiates a malevolent hiss or hum. It is an experience of pure evil. It is an experience of utter nothingness, but it is something and it is very real. It does not come from anything, but it will not go away. It is repulsive and abhorrent, but it seems to suck you in. Later in life, in the Gospel of Mark, I would come across the horrible New Testament Greek phrase *to blēdygma tēs erēmōseōs*, the abomination of desolation. That phrase struck me as coming very close to describing the object of my recurring nightmare. The object encapsulated fear, but it was deeper than fear, a hopelessness deeper than despair. It was the pure form or manifestation of utter desolation. I would wake up from this nightmare utterly exhausted and trembling. I never told anyone about this phenomenon.

The truth is I never told anyone about anything. Everything was to be kept to myself, for fear of ... for fear of what? Of humiliation, embarrassment, rejection.

One thing I did try to tell my mother and father about many times was what I called 'feeling dizzy.' I cannot blame them for failing to understand or connect with what I was trying to say. 'Feeling dizzy' did not mean anything to them and from my own point of view was a quite inadequate description of what I would experience. This phenomenon was triggered by sudden loud noise, or excessive silence, or by anything repetitive or continuous, like the ticking of a clock. Most especially it was brought on by anything that went round and round, or any sound or phrase that repeated itself. I know why I called it feeling dizzy because it brought on a sort of vertigo. What I was experiencing was a form of panic attack. Any repetitive motion or sound, a pendulum would be a perfect example, would send me into a panicking sense of losing my mind. Watching a children's swing, or being on a swing, could also be very painful for me. Visiting the famous *Rheinfall* waterfall in Schaffhausen was supposed to be a major treat for us as a day trip from Freiburg. It was agony for me. As I experienced the continuous flow of water I was filled with horror and had to work hard to keep control and stop my mind tumbling into panic. This problem has stayed with me throughout my life.

King's Drive was not centrally heated. I do not think anywhere was at that time. It would go so cold on some winter nights that when we woke up, we would find the window completely frosted over with the most incredible patterns of frost resulting from our overnight breath.

Maurice did not like being confined to the house. He loved the open air and always wanted to escape. He was very good at making porridge and sometimes just the two of us would go down together for an early breakfast. Maurice was also an expert at making cheese on toast. One day we planned to get up early and make a slice of cheese on toast and take it outside and eat it in the open air. We set off together round the block, munching the delicious snack, crossing the road opposite the house to Westgate, turning left at Regent's Drive, then left at Eastgate, and then left at the sub-station to go back home along King's Drive. We never sought permission for any such escapades and were never questioned upon our return. I would never have done anything like this if it had not been for Maurice. Strolling along in the freshness of the early morning sunshine and the tranquil peacefulness of the familiar streets, with Maurice chatting away and pointing out and commenting on things of interest as we passed, was the very epitome of freedom and sophistication. Cheese on toast had never tasted so good, and never would again.

On our way home from St Pius X, Maurice and I would sometimes cross the Garstang Road early so that we could walk on the other side. Off the Garstang Road on that side was a large crescent hidden by enormous mature trees and containing an impressive row of huge Victorian houses. Three enormous red brick and stone semis fronted onto the Garstang Rd, hidden behind trees. Within the crescent were two more huge Victorian mansions, surrounded by trees and lawns. This street was called The Nooklands. We regarded it as a place of considerable prestige and wealth. Maurice and I could gain access to one of the houses because it was the residence of a very nice friend of ours called Swarbrick. He would invite us in for a while on our way home. We always took him up on the offer, in the hope of cadging something to eat. This lad was so rich that he could afford to hand out Blue Ribands. These delicious, luxurious treats were never seen in the Mohan household.

After Maurice had gone to Preston Catholic College, I had to walk to and from school on my own. After school, I liked to cross the road early because it avoided the humiliation of having to be allowed across by the lollipop man, and you could also take a short cut home through Regent's Drive.

I used to see two beautiful Chow Chow dogs being taken for a walk up Garstang Road. They had dense coats of rough white hair and their bright purple tongues were always hanging out. One day as I walked up past the Nooklands I saw the two Chow Chow dogs break free from their leads and run madly across the busy road and through the lanes of speeding cars. One of them made it to my side of the road and arrived just near me. I looked up to see a car strike the other dog, which flew through the air. The dog next to me turned back, only to see his companion lying lifeless and covered in blood in the middle of the road. He rushed to the other dog's side and tried to lick and paw his companion to life. He let out a howl of pain and grief that I would never forget.

The sub-station was the scene of a famous picnic, instigated by my younger sister Bernadette, who was very enterprising. She wanted to go on an adventure and organised some food and snacks, presumably with Mum's help, and took a picnic blanket with her. I do not know who accompanied her, but I do not think a parent was involved. Bernadette must have been about 4 or 5 years old. I know I was not very nice to my sister Bernadette because I can remember chasing her aggressively all the way from the hall, through the morning room, to the kitchen. Mum was standing in the little alcove at the end of the kitchen, wearing her post-war apron / overall and cooking on the Creda stove. Bernadette was screaming in fear and clinging on to Mum's legs and hiding herself in the folds of Mum's apron. 'You two are like cats and dogs. *Hör auf. Sei nicht so ungezogen!*' Bernadette was never aggressive or difficult in any way and there was no need for me to be chasing her like that.

On the wall of the morning room there was a set of prints by George Hann. These Mediterranean town and village scenes were the height of fashion at the time and a sign of good taste and well-travelled sophistication. On the wall of the lounge was a large black and white plate in the style of Picasso. I thought this was very disturbing but it was also the height of fashion. On one of the triangular pull-out coffee tables rested the famous wedding gift, the little brown jug.

Our television was a magnificent model set in a highly polished cabinet. It could be glided around on wheels and had double opening doors, with classical brass pendants for handles. It was rented from Radio Rentals and had a Bakelite vertical hold knob, which we had to use to stop the picture from travelling endlessly upwards. Throughout our childhood Mum had an iron routine which was that after lunch she went to bed for an afternoon sleep or at least a lie down.

From the very earliest age we would simply keep quiet and look after ourselves, knowing that at all costs we must not disturb her. After her nap Mum would sit and we would enjoy *Watch with Mother* for fifteen minutes. That was how we fell in love with the Woodentops, and Muffin the Mule, Bill and Ben, the Flowerpot Men and their friend Weed, Andy Pandy and Rag Tag and Bobtail.

I think we might have watched some news, because we knew that Harold Macmillan was the Prime Minister. We also knew that Selwyn Lloyd was the Chancellor and in 1962 we heard that he had introduced a very unpopular budget, which included some sort of tax on sweets. Bernadette made a big cardboard banner on which she wrote 'I like sweets but I don't like Selwyn' and stood on the patch of grass on the pavement by the silver birch in front of our house opposite the front gates. We loved the silver birch on the grass verge and regarded it as our own private property. I thought Bernadette was very brave and clever.

We also seemed to know about the Aldermaston Marches and were very impressed by the duffle-coated protesters and their walking protest. Bernadette made a large Ban the Bomb notice and again stood bravely outside the gates, making her protest to passers-by on their way to and from the Corner. We lived in permanent fear of the Yellow Peril, which would consist of a full-scale invasion and occupation of Europe and Great Britain by the Chinese. We were very aware of the Atom Bomb and fully expected that we could be blown up at any moment, a fear that became a real possibility during the Cuban Missile Crisis in the Autumn of 1962, in our last few weeks at King's Drive.

Our television also fed us with a comforting diet of American Westerns, on which almost all our games were based. We could all sing the theme tune to *Rawhide*:

Rolling, rolling, rolling.
Keep those dogies rollin',
Rawhide!
All the things I'm missin',
Livin', lovin', kissin',
Waitin' at the end of my ride.
Move 'em out, head 'em up,
Head 'em up, Move 'em out,
Rawhide!

Just as good as *Rawhide* was *Wagon Train*, which usually involved the wagons pulling together into a defensive circle, while they were attacked by Native Americans, or Red Indians as we called them then, and then being relieved by the US Cavalry. The finest Western was definitely *Bonanza*, with its fascinating Cartwright family living on the *Ponderosa*.

We must have watched 'The Other Side' at times, because we did get to know some of the TV advertising jingles. We could all sing

'I'm the Veno's Snowman, call me Pop.
You'll find me in the Chemist's shop.
When you take Veno's, your cough soon goes,
So stop that cough with …
Veno's!'

We could also recite simple advertising lines such as *'Tense, nervous headache? Nothing acts faster than Anadin!'* or *'Have a Break, Have a Kit Kat!'* We all knew that Kellogg's Ricicles were twicicles as nicicles, and that Rice Krispies went Snap, Crackle and Pop!

In 1960 a lady called Dr Barbara Moore decided to walk from John O'Groats to Land's End. Each evening we would follow her progress on the news. When she walked through Preston, Edmund and his classmates at Preston Catholic College were made to line the route and cheer as the long-distance walker went past.

One day Dad decided to redecorate the front room and so he stripped off the wall paper. We children enjoyed soaking the paper and scraping it off in long pieces. An extraordinary thing happened. When we had scraped off the paper on the right-hand wall of the lounge, the wall with the dining room or back room on the other side, we found the name Mohan written on the plaster.

There were two favourite recreation places where we could be guaranteed to meet up with large numbers of children from the local area. Both locations were equally hazardous. One was the railway line, which could be accessed by the side of the bridge on the Cadley Causeway, just before you got to St Antony's. The other was the air raid shelter on the other side of Black Bull Lane, just up from the Corner.

This was a very large concrete bomb shelter in the form of a long passageway set underground, with steps at each end. It was full of broken glass and cans and smelled of urine. We hung around there feeling connected to the excitement of the Second World War. All around it was a derelict wasteland, ideal for playing games and looking for scraps of wood. The air raid shelter was a favourite place for us to play and here we would meet large numbers of other children from the surrounding area whom we did not actually know. Our parents never questioned us as to where we had been and never gave us any warnings to stay away from the air raid shelter.

Sometimes as we walked along King's Drive on our way to school, we would pass the road sweeper. He had a rectangular barrow made of metal, with metal lids on top and brackets where he could put his shovel and brush. Our favourite game was to pick up the largest stone or rock we could find and lob it into his metal barrow as we passed. It would make a mighty clang as it hit the metal. We would run off screaming with laughter and would turn round to see him shaking his fist and brandishing his broom. He had a grey cap and a grubby brown suit. He was simple man and this was undoubtedly very cruel.

Occasionally, as we walked up King's Drive, a Messerschmitt bubble car would come chugging past. This was an extraordinary vehicle, with two wheels at the front and one at the back. It could accommodate two people, but they had to sit in tandem, one behind the other. The Messerschmitt aeroplane company was not allowed to make aeroplanes in the post-war years and so had to turn temporarily to automobile manufacturing. The result was this motor that looked just like an aeroplane that had lost its wings. The model we would see belonged to the father of a boy called Gabriel Masonnier, whose family was of Hungarian origin.

We were allowed to wander far and wide without our parents' permission or knowledge. The Stoats and Rabbits was the name Veronica gave to one of the special places we went to, out in the countryside, far from buildings and houses. Here there were trees, fields, and a stream. I do not know where this was. I am not even sure that I ever went there. But I know that Veronica would speak of it as a magical kingdom into which they had escaped and always wanted to return to and recapture.

While living in Preston, we seemed to have very little to do with Dad's family, even though we were not living too far from them. I do remember that we once visited and stayed with Dad's sister, Aunty Kit, her husband Sydney and their three children, Christopher, Josephine, and Gerard in the North East somewhere. I think we stayed there overnight because we were there for the evening and sat and listened to Sydney playing the piano, especially the tune *Happy Days are Here Again*.

Rare Mohan family group photo – occasion and location unknown
Everyone is wearing Sunday best
Mum, Bernadette in Bavarian costume, Edmund, Francis with bow tie, Maurice with snake belt, Dad with his sisters Eileen, Kit and Frances, our grandmother Catherine Lee, Veronica.

I do recall just one visit to Middlesborough to see our grandmother Catherine Lee. On the way we went through Brighouse and called on Kit and Sydney, who had moved from the North East and were living there at the time. I thought this town was rather horrible, because we seemed to pass through a very narrow, claustrophobic valley and all the stone houses seemed to be pitch black with smoke and grime. The Hill family lived on the slopes above the town.

Christopher and Gerard and Josie were older now and came across as impossibly sophisticated. We sat with them in the garden, while the parents spoke inside. The two brothers showed off a dry-stone wall they had built and Chris showed us some black and white photos he had taken. They were our only British cousins, but we did not know them at all and the age difference meant there was little point of connection. The garden was sloping and had been made into a series of terraces.

The drive over the Yorkshire Moors was very impressive and Dad told us that as a young boy he had cycled all over these moors. It was pitch dark as we came off the high ground and began to descend towards Middlesborough. We were met with the awesome sight of the Dorman Long Steel Works, belching fire and smoke out into the night sky and lighting up the town. We knew that our grandfather, Francis Mohan, had worked as a steelworker at the legendary engineering and steel plant and were proud of the fact that our grandfather had worked for the company that had built the Tyne and the Sydney Harbour bridges.

18 Rockliffe Road had a tiny garden at the front to separate it from the road and a bay window at the front on both the ground and the first floor, putting it in a higher social bracket than the standard Victorian terrace. Nothing seemed to happen in the front room and life seemed to go on in the middle room or parlour, next to the kitchen. It must have been 1957 or 1958, because I was old enough to remember these few details. My grandmother died in 1961, without me ever really knowing her or her knowing me in any meaningful way. She was 80 in 1958 and died in January 1961. I have no memory of Dad or us attending a funeral.

Peter Johnson lived on the same side of King's Drive as us in a smart semi-detached house. His father was the manager of the newly opened 'drive-in' branch of the Trustees Savings Bank, the very epitome of the prosperous new world that was opening all around us. We called him Jeeter Ponson. He was famous for having dropped and smashed a jar of marmalade right on the pavement outside our house, I think we helped to clear it up. He was then sent back to the Corner by his parents on another occasion, charged with the same shopping errand. He was very well spoken and as he walked past with his second jar of marmalade he said 'You know, the last time I went to get one of these I jettisoned it.' This became something we would often say as we went about the house or set or cleared the table.

Peter Johnson was something of a fantasist and told us in all seriousness that he was in the process of constructing a helicopter at the back of his house in King's Drive. With a straight face and complete conviction, he said to Mum 'You know, once it's finished, I can take you over to Germany to visit your mother.' 'Yes Peter, I would like that very much,' replied Mum, with perfect courtesy and an equally straight face.

I knew that at Preston Catholic College, if a teacher wanted to punish a pupil by means of the cane or rod, which was completely normal and accepted in those days, that teacher had to issue the offender with a chit, stating the number of blows to be received, so that the offender could report at morning break or lunchtime and present the chit at the punishment office to whoever of the Jesuits was on punishment duty that day.

Dad used to take sandwiches to Preston Catholic College and Mum used to make them for him. Sometimes she would make him a fried egg sandwich and he really liked this. I pestered Mum and asked her if she would make a fried egg sandwich for me to take to St Pius X for lunch. She did as I asked but it did not turn out well. Eating the cold and greasy fried egg made me feel sick and I was not able to finish it. In addition, my fellow pupils were horrified by the sight and smell and were very rude about my sandwiches. My attempt to be like Dad had failed.

If you went upstairs at King's Drive and turned right at the top of the stairs, the toilet was on your right. It was the only toilet in the house. If you carried on past the toilet you came to the small family bathroom at the end of the landing. As you entered the bathroom immediately ahead of you was the door to the airing cupboard. This was a favourite place to hide during hide and seek. Dad installed a new copper hot water tank with a new immersion heater in it. He bought some 2" by 1" and made two slatted shelves for storing the sheets and towels. As you turned right into the bathroom, the bath was on your left and the wash basin straight ahead. This is where we would wash ourselves every night, following Mum's strict rule of Hands, Face, Neck, Ears, Knees, Teeth.

I used to sit on the bath near the taps and watch Dad shave in the morning at the weekend. He would sing Danny Boy in a strong, loud voice and I would watch the shavings being shaken off into the hot water. The shaving cream was in a big tub made of opaque white glass with a screw top lid. Dad would apply it with a proper shaving brush with a polished wooden handle. He would splash Old Spice on his face at the end of the shave.

It was at that sink that I gave myself a serious injury, the scar of which I can still see on my finger today, the middle finger of my left hand. I had lots of little plastic *Airfix* soldiers and I used to love to set up battles with them In order to enhance my battle scenes I decided I should cut off the legs of one or two soldiers. I turned the screw handle of Dad's smart metal razor. The folding shields opened at the top and I carefully removed the Wilkinson Sword blade. I held the soldier in my left hand, between my index finger and thumb and proceeded to saw at the soldier's leg with the razor blade held in my right hand. When I sawed through the soldier's leg, the razor blade sliced straight down onto my middle finger and very nearly sliced the whole of the top joint off. I ran down to Mum screaming and she had to be very quick and careful in order to stem the flow of bleeding. I perhaps should have had stitches, but we did not bother with any medical intervention. The finger remained tightly bound with regular changes of dressings for days. I did not get told off or reprimanded in any way for my foolhardiness.

When we lived in Preston, Dad had a lovely blue tweed jacket. It was a beautiful powder blue and suited him very well. He would often wear it when he went for walks on a Sunday afternoon. He was of a generation that did not really have many casual or summer clothes. For many years his favourite short-sleeved shirt was what we called his wasp shirt. It was bright yellow with black stripes. The material was very thin and shiny, like rayon or nylon.

Dad never liked to spend on himself and was not really interested in how he looked or dressed. However, when we lived in Preston Mum and Dad must have been in the money and decided to go out one day and treat themselves to beautiful new expensive winter coats. Dad's was a very fine dark black wool overcoat, with Raglan sleeves and a large fold-down collar. Just after buying it Mum and Dad went out to a very posh do, something to do with either school or church. I do not know exactly what happened but that night, just a few days after he had bought it, Dad's expensive new early 60s winter coat was stolen. He and Mum were crestfallen, especially as Dad could not really afford the coat in the first place.

Dad loved his sandals. Like his army shorts, these were for him a symbol of freedom and summer happiness. Dad was always trying to find the perfect pair of sandals. Once in the summer he treated himself to yet another pair of sandals and bequeathed to me his old pair. I can still feel what my feet felt like in Dad's sandals. His left foot twisted down on the left onto its outside edge. He had quite bad feet with prominent bunions.

Of great fascination to us as children was the hard lump sticking out from the side of Dad's right shin. Enclosed under a shiny mound of flesh and sunk into his bone was a lump of shrapnel, which had struck him during the war and which the medics must have decided was not worth removing.

Like most little children, when I was pre-school, I was always falling and grazing or cutting my knees. I fell very heavily one day and got a very deep cut in my knee. Mum sorted me out in the bathroom and then sat me on the edge of her bed. She gave me a German chocolate wrapped in foil and told me that this would soon make it better. She went off to do her chores and came back an hour later, to find me still rubbing the chocolate on my knee, hoping I was doing it in the right way to heal the cut.

Once I was put in the front bedroom above the porch for an afternoon sleep. I was aged four. I could not sleep but I made a game for myself. I had the tin lid from a Quality Street tin. When I turned it upside down there was a channel all around the circumference. I had two marbles and put them in the channel. My game was to tilt the lid skilfully so that the marbles went round and round. Part of the game was to accelerate and then decelerate the marbles. But the most challenging part was to make sure that the marbles never touched. I would sit up in bed and watch for what seemed like hours on end.

Dad was famously strict and quick to anger, but also ridiculously lax and tolerant at others, on the whole exercising almost no supervision over us at all. Once Dad took us out for a drive and pulled in at a sort of layby, where there had been a lot of fly-tipping. We boys rooted around in the rubbish, looking for interesting items. We soon found a leather car seat, almost intact. We asked Dad if we could put it in the car and take it home with us and he, to our surprise, readily agreed. When we got back home, we had great fun with this car seat. Edmund was always interested in aeroplanes and soon convinced us that its best use would be as a pretend fighter jet ejector seat. Edmund and Maurice carried it to the rockery at the bottom of the garden and placed it carefully at the summit of the slope, which consisted of substantial boulders and stones. I was very proud when they chose me to be the honoured person who would be accorded the privilege of trialling the ejector seat. I was strapped to the seat and a motorcycle crash helmet, which was far too large for me, was balanced precariously on my head.

On the count of three I was tipped forward, to roll down the eight or ten feet of the rockery slope. Within seconds I was screaming and howling, as the whole of my front and my arms were reduced to a mass of cuts and bruises. I do not recall anyone being reprimanded for this escapade and I think that Dad was quite happy for us to learn our own lessons.

The rockery was also the scene of another famous incident of cruelty. This time the victim was my younger sister Bernadette and I was one of the co-conspirators. We had learned how to create a man-trap by digging a large hole and by then covering the large hole with an interlocking lattice of frail twigs. The twigs were then covered with one layer of newspaper, which was in turn covered with a layer of soil, all finished off to look as natural as possible. We asked Bernadette if she would like to come on an adventure. We led her through the garden and made her follow us up the rockery, carefully stepping over the trap ourselves and leading her to fall suddenly into the hole. Bernadette was not stupid and knew something was up right from the start. She went along with the trick out of curiosity and just so that she could take part. Sometimes we were not very nice to Bernadette. We knew that she had a phobia of 'fluffies' and so we sometimes decided it would be fun to frighten her with them. A 'fluffy' was a little feather that might be found lying on the floor or floating in the air. This feather down used to come out of the awful black and white striped pillows we used at the time. The idea was to find a fluffy and let it float down near Bernadette, then laugh when she screamed and ran away.

Bernadette, standing on the rockery, with someone behind her

To the left of the rockery, at the bottom of the garden, behind a rustic arch and hidden by some bushes, were the remains of the concrete domestic air raid shelter. It was a frightening place to go and Dad used the trough between the concrete slabs as a place to put all his grass clippings.

Dad used to run trips to Germany for the boys from Preston Catholic College. He knew this was the only way to bring the German language to life and he also wanted to foster understanding and reconciliation between cultures and nations. On one of Dad's rail trips to Germany he had a very difficult boy, not badly behaved but naïve and unpredictable. As the train pulled into the station in Germany, Dad was shocked to see this boy open the carriage door and hurl himself out of the train screaming 'First one on German soil!' This same boy spent almost all his spending money on a gift to take home to his mother. It was a wooden box entirely covered with shells. It was so awful that Dad felt terribly sorry for him.

Easter Sunday in the garden at King's Drive
Veronica, Maurice, Edmund, Bernadette

On one of his trips Dad hired a rowing boat on a mountain lake and decided to have a swim. He dived off the boat into the lake and just kept on going down and down. It felt as if there was nothing he could do about it. He thought he would never actually find the strength to reverse his direction and make his way back up to the surface. He would recall this as one of the most frightening experiences of his life.

When Dad returned from his school trips it was very exciting because he would bring back presents for all us children. The best present he ever brought back for me was a beautiful padded leather documents case, with a zip round three sides and various compartments for money and passports and elastic holders for pens and pencils. Another amazing present was a beautiful black and gold Schaeffer fountain pen with a semi-italic nib. Dad was away from home quite a lot when we lived in Preston because he was also a representative for the NUT and would attend their annual conference. He was not particularly militant, but I think he thought that if he was to advance in his career it would be very useful to gain some understanding and experience of the political side of school and staffroom life. At King's Drive I was once standing in the hallway and chatting to Dad, who was standing near the front door. I got no response so I looked up to see a young man standing politely, leather briefcase in hand. As well as the extra teaching at the girls' convent at Winckley Square, Dad was doing private tuition to earn a bit of extra cash. He always had a tendency to take on too much.

One day at King's Drive we got back from Mass, only to find that we had locked ourselves out. A solution was found when Dad noticed a small window had been left open in the little rectangular bay that stuck out from the morning room at the side of the house. Dad hoisted me up and fed me through the window head first. I then scrambled down and along to the kitchen door to let everyone in. I was the hero of the hour.

A less glorious moment occurred when some friends came round to visit us. They had a boy of my age. I took against him because he had an unpleasant face, but the last straw was when he commandeered my tricycle. I got his bare arm and sunk my teeth into it. I was quite astonished but also very impressed to see a perfect set of teeth marks in his arm, from which blood began to seep. He howled the place down; his parents came out of the house through the French windows and were so disgusted that they left immediately.

Mum was forced to pursue them out of the house mumbling that 'This was quite out of character' or words to that effect. Neither Mum nor Dad told me off or punished me in any way. In fact, I think they were quite happy to see the back of their visitors. This incident took place on the grey sloping concrete terrace or patio which led down from the French windows to the broad steps into the garden. This was where we would spend hours riding around on our tricycles, scooters, and bikes.

One time at King's Drive, when I really did get told off was an unfortunate incident which left me very shaken indeed. I had been invited to a birthday party and I was given some Victoria sponge cake to take home. When we got home, I went to the morning room and got it out on the black shiny table. Mum started cutting it up so that she could share it out among my brothers and sisters. I complained about this and said the cake was really mine. Dad witnessed this and went absolutely mad. He screamed and shouted and hit me. He completely lost his temper and finished by taking the cake and pushing it into my mouth saying 'There you are! Now you can eat all the cake you want and see how you like it.' One of the curious things about Dad's punishments was that they were always accompanied by the repeated expression 'I'll give you something to cry about,' as if he was surprised and annoyed that beating us was resulting in us crying and as if we were not crying enough already. When Dad smeared the cake in my face I felt total shock, accompanied by utter humiliation, but also by a feeling of pity for Dad that he should behave in this way towards me.

I must now mention the rose-pruning incident, one of the most heinous crimes I committed at King's Drive. There is not much to tell. One sunny spring day I decided to prune the roses. As was very common in the 1950s, the back garden in King's Drive had a beautiful circular traditional flowerbed, with a very fine collection of roses, typical of gardens at that time. I got a large pair of scissors from the kitchen and snipped off every one of the buds. Mum had her customary sleep in the afternoon and on that day she got up from her sleep and came down to find her rose collection destroyed. She screamed in shock. I thought I was doing something good and helpful. Once again, neither Mum nor Dad was truly angry with me and I received no punishment.

Dad himself could never be described as a gardener. Like many men, he was much more at home with hacking things down than with cultivating them. One day, he proudly came home from a gardening shop with a white roll of material in a plastic covering and a large label in lurid colours. The label proclaimed that this was the Magic Carpet. The illustration on the cover showed a man rolling out the carpet on a flower bed, while a fabulous display of beautiful blooms sprung up instantaneously. All you had to do was water it. It was a huge roll of double layered tissue paper, with hundreds of flowers seeds trapped between the two layers. Not a single bloom ever emerged and for months the surface of the flower beds was covered with a soggy mass of white tissue paper.

The flower beds where Dad had so optimistically laid his magic carpet lay between two rhododendron bushes along the hedge between ourselves and Mrs Bilsborrow. Once in the summer our football went over into Mrs Bilsborrow's so Maurice and I crawled through the gap in the hedge to retrieve it. We must have had our shirts off due to the heat, because Mum very soon received a visit from an outraged Mrs Bilsborrow, who told Mum that she had looked out of her back window to see 'naked bodies' running around her grounds. Although it was the 1950s, Mrs Bilsborrow had her house furnished in the style of the 1890s, with heavy mahogany furniture piled up with lace coverings and silver framed photos and vases and knick-knacks. Once when I was little Mum took me round with her for an afternoon cup of tea with Mrs Bilsborrow. I knew that I had to keep absolutely still and silent as Mrs Bilsborrow looked at me with undisguised distaste. Throughout her life, no matter where she lived, Mum was very good at keeping on good terms with her neighbours. Towards the end of her life, it was a matter of pride to her that she had never fallen out with her neighbours and she advised us all to follow her example.

The same stretch of flowerbed, between the rhododendrons, was also the scene of a plumbing emergency. The water mains pipes below the bed somehow ruptured and a gaping hole, rapidly filling with water, appeared where the bed had once been. When the plumbers arrived, there was great excitement, as Dad informed us that they were none other than Preston North End legend Tom Finney, together with his brother Joe. We all stood round gaping at them as they worked, trying to absorb the fact that we were standing so close to someone 'Famous'. In truth, the full import of the moment was somewhat lost on us, given the fact that none of us, including Dad, had the slightest interest in, or knowledge of, footballing matters.

The other side of our semi was occupied by Molly and Peggy who together cared for a young boy called Ralph Cairns. Who Ralph was, and why he was living with Molly and Peggy, was a mystery. They were too old for one of them to be his mother so they must have undertaken to look after him for someone else. The curly-haired Ralph was fun to be with as he was always up to no good and getting himself into scrapes. His head was full of silly ideas and he liked to spin yarns. Molly and Peggy were always despairing of him and could not really cope. They seemed to aspire to be a cut above and had a fine display of Doulton figures on the window sill of their bay window.

At the back of our houses, running along the back of King's Drive, there was a farm. The farm still had a lovely orchard of apples and pears. One of our favourite sports or dares was to venture through the back hedge into the farm to scrump apples and pears. One day Ralph Cairns and I saw a beautiful cart horse on the other side of the hedge and decided it would be fun to feed him some bread. Ralph duly popped home and came back the proud bearer of half a loaf of fresh white slice bread, swiped from under the noses of Molly and Peggy. We broke through the hedge and the slices of bread were promptly accepted and eaten by the horse. Ralph was holding the bread wrapping, which in those days consisted of heavy waxed paper. The horse unexpectedly lurched forward to get some bread, took the whole bread wrapping into its mouth and gulped it down. Ralph and I were shocked and made a dash for it. We were utterly convinced that the waxed paper would be the death of the horse and went back every day for a week to see if it was still alive. Not only did the horse survive, but Ralph never received any comeback from Molly and Peggy for the theft of the loaf of bread.

The back garden at King's Drive, showing the rockery and the hedge at the back through which we fed the horse.

The garage can be seen on the right.

On the other side of the hedge are the farm buildings and the orchard.

Mum was a very good cook. She taught herself all the standard English dishes, such as roast beef and Yorkshire pudding, roast potatoes, gravy, apple pie and so on. But she also held on to her German culture. And so we were brought up with all sorts of wonderful foreign foods, of which our English friends and acquaintances had not the faintest idea. One of her specialities was rissoles, which took her all morning to make. They were rounded patties or meat balls and were based on the famous *Königsberger Klopse*. Mum would always make extras so that some could be saved and eaten cold later, smothered with German mustard. When Mum made mashed potatoes, she would put a large block of butter into a pan and fry it until it was completely brown and sizzling, so that we could pour it all over our potatoes. One of Mum's legendary dishes was very simple but we all loved it; 'Macaroni and Prunes'. The prunes would be soaked and cooked so that they were sitting in a gloopy, sweet sauce, which we would pour over a plate of macaroni. Mum would then mix sugar with cinnamon and we would sprinkle this generously on top of the prunes. Throughout her life one of Mum's signature dishes was a sort of pea and ham soup, made from scratch from green split peas. Instead of ham hock, the thick pea soup would have generous chunks of *Bockwurst*. It would be seasoned with Marmite and Maggi *Würze*. Frankfurters were always a popular standby and we would eat any amount of these, again covered in German mustard or *Senf*. We would happily have *Sauerkraut* with our mashed potatoes and loved the taste of caraway seeds or *Kümmel*. Mum would mix little pieces of chopped up bacon into the *Sauerkraut*, just to make it even more delicious. Her *Bratkartoffeln* were nothing like the English version. They were cut quite thick and fried with little pieces of bacon. When Mum baked a cake, it was always in a loaf tin, rather than a circular cake tin. She had three standard cakes, all of them excellent, a lemon drizzle, a fruit cake, and a German-style chocolate marble cake.

We were the only family we knew who would have lengthy Sunday breakfasts, with finger rolls, brie, camembert, and salami. We would never call it salami; we just called it *Wurst*. Mum and Dad's two favourite wurst-styles were *Cervelat* and Garlic Wurst. These were not purchased in sealed pre-packed cellophane packets of salami slices. Instead, Mum and Dad bought a whole large sausage and enjoyed keeping it for days and even weeks, slicing it exactly to their own preferred thickness. We also had *Leberwurst* or liver pâté, as well as Austrian smoked cheese spread. Without a doubt Mum's favourite delicacy was Roll Mop Herrings, skewered with cocktail sticks and filled with whole black peppercorns.

They gave her a taste of home, of the famous Königsberger *Rollmopse* or 'Bismarck Herrings'. We would have *Pumpernickel*, the dark black slices of rich rye bread. Nobody explained to us at the time that '*pumpern*' was German for 'to poop' and that this bread was reputed to have this unfortunate side-effect. We also had Quark cheese to spread on our Pumpernickel, at a time when no-one in England had ever heard of either of these items. Long before the term 'delicatessen' came into general use, Mum and Dad had discovered a top-quality delicatessen in Preston run by a Polish emigré by the name of Mr Kasperek. It was from there that they got so many of these cherished reminders of the East, including authentic German *Brotchen* and poppy seed rolls.

Edmund and I wrestling on the tyres. Photograph probably set up and taken by Fr Monk.

We also looked forward to Sunday evening tea, which had a more English feel to it. We would have a nice white crusty farmhouse loaf, which Dad would cut into slices as required. There would be a large square block of pure white Lancashire cheese, moist and crumbly and very sharp on the tongue. We would cover this with Pan Yan Pickle or with Sandwich Spread.

We had lots of 'Things to Put on Bread'. Honey, Globus Jam from Eastern Europe. Kraft cheese slices, Dairy Lea triangles. Mum would slice tomatoes up and make a bowl of finely diced onion. We would then cover a slice of buttered bread with tomato slices and cover them with the diced raw onion. We would then cover the onion with black pepper. It often seemed to happen that while eating this Dad would either laugh or sneeze and the whole table would be sprayed with peppery fragments of diced onion. We were one of the few families at this time to know about gherkins. Other 'Things to Put on Bread' were fish paste, salmon paste and crab paste, the last one in a lovely thick white shiny pot. Mum would put a block of dates on the table, all compacted into a rectangular block. We would slice this like cheese and put it on our bread. A home-made thing to put on bread would be fat from frying bacon. Mum would collect this in a bowl and we would then spread it cold on our bread, sprinkling it generously with salt. We would also have tins of Molasses and Lyle's Golden Syrup which we would spread on our bread. A typical teatime dessert might be some Swiss Roll, or some peaches with evap. Alternatively we might have Birds Instant Whip or Angel Delight, especially Raspberry or Butterscotch flavoured, which Mum allowed us to sprinkle with desiccated coconut. This was delicious and you were especially lucky if the powder had not dissolved fully and you hit a few little pockets of the original sweet powder. Sometimes on Sunday our dessert would be baked apples. The core was removed and filled with sultanas which swelled up in the oven. On Bonfire Night Mum made amazing Parkin with lots of ginger, molasses, and oatmeal.

Preston was a port, with an unusual harbour built on the side of the river, quite close to the centre of town. On New Year's Eve, we boys and girls would stay awake in our beds so that we could listen to the noise of all the ships at the port sounding their horns to welcome in the New Year. It was an eery and mysterious sound, but at the same time comforting, and a shared experience.

On the New Year's Eve of 1959, I was 7 years old. I knew from school that the decade of the 1950s was over and that in the morning it would be 1960, the start of a new year and a new decade. I should have been looking forward to this bright new decade with great excitement. I could not have known that it would turn out to be one of the most momentous decades in history. But I was not excited. Instead, I wept. I lay in bed crying. I was desperately upset that the years were disappearing into the past. I knew how happy I had been and that I would never be as happy again.

Chapter 16

Newquay

And Pike's morass

In the summer of 1962 Dad took us on holiday to Newquay in Cornwall. We camped at the northern end of Newquay, using Porth Beach as our base. We spent most of our time there playing with the cheap plywood surfing boards popular at the time. We thought Newquay was a paradise and an incredible escape from Lancashire. On the way down to Newquay we stopped for a day or two at a sort of farm or roadside campsite which we just called Pike's and which was run by Mr and Mrs Pike.

The Pike's campsite, if it can be called that, was situated on the road over the hills north of Bath. The A46, which ran North-South from Stroud to Bath, had a crossroads with the A420, running West-East from Chippenham to Bristol. The Pike land was not far from this crossroads as you carried on south in the direction of Bath. It had once been a functioning farm, but the agricultural activities had been reduced as Mr and Mrs Pike got older. They now survived on a combination of campsite and café. The café was an old-fashioned, smoke-filled shack, with steamed-up windows, tacked onto the front of the farmhouse. The fare consisted of various combinations of sausage, egg, bacon, and beans. The 'camp site' was a hillocky, sloping, muddy field, exposed to wind and rain, with no road or track and no facilities to speak of. For the toilet and for washing we went to one simple WC and sink in a grubby outhouse at the back of the farmhouse. In order to get the most level land possible, our tents had to be pitched high up at the brow of the hill above the farmhouse, where there was maximum exposure to the elements. If you went down the hill slope towards the main road there was a huge section of long, dark-green grass, covering a filthy. muddy bog. Dad named this area The Morass and told us to keep away from it, guessing that this was the destination of the drained waste from the house. There was nothing to do at Pike's, no play area and nowhere to walk or explore and not a single tree in sight. It appealed to Dad because it could be reached in a day's drive from Preston, plus it was cheap. Perhaps more importantly, Dad loved the simple life and Pike's appealed to him as a place of freedom and informality.

Amazingly, while staying for a few days at Pike's, Dad drove us down into Bath one evening and paid for us all to attend the Bath Tattoo. This was a hugely impressive experience for us children. It was the first time we had been out together to such a huge public event, at night, with thousands of people. It took place on the Recreation Ground, a large, flat, open space close to the river in the centre of Bath. The Tattoo started with Community Singing. We were issued with leaflets containing all the words of the songs, such as 'It's a Long Way to Tipperary'. After the community singing and marching bands, there was an interval and we went to the toilets. The men's urinals were housed in a large canvas tent and consisted of recycled oil barrels. Men had to stand around the oil drum in a circle and urinate into a huge vat of urine. I found this quite traumatic, especially as it was almost impossible to reach over the height of the drum.

The main part of the tattoo consisted of breath-taking gymnastic displays by the army, navy, and air force troops, followed by motorcycle stunts, unarmed combat, ground attack routines, jeep manoeuvres and shooting skills. I thought the whole thing was marvellous and could not believe that we had been given such a treat. I went to my bed in my tent that night dreaming of Victor-esque combat missions and military exploits. We saved our word sheets and all the way down to Newquay we lightened the journey with our community songs.

While we were staying at Pike's, something else happened that would signal a turning point in our lives. Dad went off very smartly dressed one morning and drove from the boggy marsh of the camp-site to the centre of Bristol. It was only when he returned at the end of the day that we realised that he had been attending an interview for the Headship of a secondary modern school. After just a one-day selection process he was appointed as Headteacher of St Thomas More's School, situated on Stottbury Road in Horfield. Horfield was a relatively deprived area of Bristol, situated between Redland and the Gloucester Road. Horfield was a well-known name because it was the location of Bristol's prison. Dad returned home to Pike's late in the afternoon and was jubilant with his success. The school had been built at the end of the war, following the 1944 Education Act. At that time Catholic grammar schools and independent schools were all run by religious orders, and it was always from the religious orders that the headteachers were chosen. Dad was ambitious and realised that the only way he could progress above Head of Department would be to move into the Secondary Modern sector. He had already done this in Preston by leaving Preston Catholic College and becoming Deputy Head of Blessed Edmund Campion School.

In his reference for Dad for the post at St Thomas More, the headteacher of Blessed Edmund Campion had written 'I shall be very sorry to lose Mr Mohan, but I have always known that it would only be a matter of time before he would want a school of his own.' The Education Department at that time was housed on College Green in the vast curving sweep of the Council House. This building had been designed in the 1930s, but was not completed until after the war and was only opened by Queen Elizabeth in 1956. Dad strode confidently past the statue of John Cabot and into the building, carrying a copy of The Guardian under his arm. A member of the interviewing panel came out to greet him and spotted the newspaper. Dad was very pleased to hear him say 'Well, there's a man who's gone up in my estimation straightaway.'

Dad was thrilled with his appointment. After he told us, we three boys took our football and had a kickaround on the sloping field. To our great surprise, Dad got up and came over to join in the game. He ran around the field with us in the summer evening sunshine, kicking, and running and passing the ball. This must have been the first and the last time he did anything like this. I remember experiencing a complicated feeling of pride and joy, mixed with discomfort and embarrassment.

We motored on from Pike's to Newquay for what I remember as an idyllic family summer holiday. We did not give the move much thought. None of it was real to us. But Dad's day at the Council House in Bristol was to change all our lives, for better or for worse, forever.

The trip to Newquay was made not in Growler, but in the Lincoln, Dad's latest, and perhaps his craziest motor vehicle. The Lincoln, registration KLF 7, was a left-hand drive, all-American classic, with vast mudguards at the front and an elegant sloping profile to the rear. An enormous, rocket-like bonnet (or 'hood') seemed to go on forever at the front, forging along the roads in stately manner like the prow of a mighty ship. In colour the Lincoln was the deepest of dark blues. Beneath the bonnet purred and roared an enormous V12 engine. Soft suspension, sloppy power-assisted steering, supple and luxurious leather seats. The beast's buffers and grille were a mass of chrome. Atop the prow rode the streamlined sliver of the Lincoln marque. If it was the 1947 model, then it was just 15 years old when Dad acquired it. Its sheer impracticality presumably lowered its price to the £10 Dad paid for it.

Already this car seemed like a creature from another world, both in space and time, a captive whale which found itself beached in a world of Triumph Heralds and Morris Minors. Our feelings about the Lincoln were ambivalent. We missed Growler, but knew deep down that his days were numbered. We felt rather privileged to be riding in what was, or at least had been, a luxury car. But we were also embarrassed, probably in the same way that we had been by Growler, who had always elicited stares and comments wherever we went. One of the most amazing features of the Lincoln was that in order to open the doors from the inside, instead of tugging on a door handle, we pushed on a large Bakelite button, set in a chrome ring. There was a series of concentric ribs on the buttons and we could never quite believe that they worked. In the summer of 1962, there was a fête and sports day at Oak House. The Lincoln swept up the gravel drive of the old house and parked up on the lawns. It was soon swarming with Pius X schoolboys, who all wanted to see this piece of floating Americana. Once in Preston there was a fair at Moor Park, closer to town just south of Fulwood. The fair was opened with a parade of American cars. On each of the vast mudguards of the cars was draped a leggy blonde in a cowboy outfit, with tiny red shorts, huge studded leather belts, fringed leather waistcoats and white Stetsons. I could hardly believe what I was seeing. This parade, the cars, and the impossibly alluring girls, summed up all the glamour we associated with America at that time.

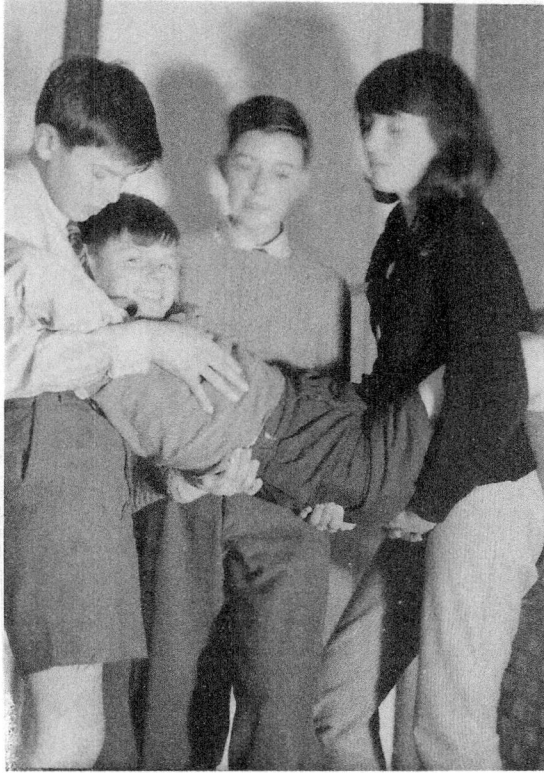

Chapter 17

Bristol

And Acker Bilk

October, 1962. An Autumn afternoon, with sun streaming in from the Victorian classroom window. I am sitting in my place at the back of the classroom, on the left. We are all looking at the huge map of Great Britain on the classroom wall, which Mr Georgeson is explaining. I am searching for Newquay on the coast of Cornwall, dreaming of the blue waves and the beautiful sandy beach. Suddenly I am jolted to attention by the mention of my name. 'And over here is Bristol, the Queen of the South, and of course that is where Francis Mohan will be moving at the end of this year.' The class shows no interest. But the prospect of moving, heard on the lips of someone else, becomes real to me for the first time.

Dad went down to Bristol on his own in advance and stayed somewhere until he had found a house. Once the house was bought, Dad moved in on his own and started work at the school from there. As the Autumn wore on, the weather became very cold. Dad wrote to us to tell us that there was a coke-burning stove and that he was sitting on top of it in the evenings to keep himself warm. Eventually, just before Christmas, the time came for us to move. Two removal men arrived at King's Drive with a very large removal van. They stayed with us for the night and we all sat on boxes in the evening and watched television with them, which I thought was very exciting. We found their accents quite comical. They were very friendly and kind to all us children. While we were watching the television, Acker Bilk came on the screen, playing *Stranger on the Shore* on his clarinet. 'ee's a Bristle man 'ee is' said the lead removal man proudly. On the day of the move, we got up early to leave the house and walk along to the bus stop where we would catch a bus to the station. As Mum walked off in the direction of the Corner, we three brothers hung back and arranged ourselves solemnly in a straight line in front of the carefully-closed front gates. We took out our cap guns, raised our right arms and fired a three-gun salute. It was our pre-arranged gesture of respect and gratitude to the house that had been our home.

I do not recall any send-offs of any kind, either at school or church, or from friends or neighbours. We were leaving behind our town, our peaceful road and neighbourhood, our beautiful parish church, our excellent schools, our friends. Dad was 44, Mum was 39, Edmund was 14 and would be 15 in January, Veronica was 13, Maurice had just turned 12 in August, I was 10, Bernadette was 9 and Madeleine was 5. Around the corner, the teenage years were waiting for us, as they would have done even had we stayed, our adolescence and the full-blown decade of the 1960s.

The six of us children travelled down from Preston to Bristol by train. We were all smartly dressed for this momentous journey, and Mum looked very elegant. We occupied our own compartment in the train, but for a large part of the journey a handsome young businessman in a sharp suit joined us. He was fascinated by us as a family and at first, he just stared at us with the same interest as someone visiting a zoo. He then started to chat to us all and played a few games to help the time to pass. He was utterly in awe of Mum and quizzed her endlessly about her and Dad and the reason for their journey. He was particularly intrigued by the economics of bringing up a large family. 'Does your husband smoke? Does your husband drink?' were two of the questions I heard him asking, which I thought was very rude. Mum dealt with the situation brilliantly. She was prim and proper, skilfully evasive, and non-committal.

The train pulled in to Temple Meads at around 5pm. We then had to find the No 2 bus stop, which would take us all the way to our new home. It was only at this point that we all got rather nervous and the prospect of facing a new home in a new town became very real. We had no idea how long the journey across the city would take, or where to get off, but eventually the bus jolted to a halt among some dark and dank Victorian houses and we looked out across the open platform of the bus to see Dad standing in his belted khaki mac, smiling and waving. We crossed the road together and walked up the right-hand side of a short, wide road, turning in to the right at the top and walking up a sloping concrete path to a large wooden porch on the right-hand side of the house. It was a freezing night. We filed in quietly, following Dad through the porch and into a large and gloomy hallway.

And there I must leave us for now, as Dad hurries off to see to the stove, and Mum makes encouraging, cheerful noises, and we begin our new life.

142

Printed in Great Britain
by Amazon